Stark County District Library
715 Market Ave. N.
Canton, OH 44702

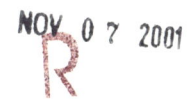

Easter Garland

Other Books by Daniel J. Foley

TOYS THROUGH THE AGES
CHRISTMAS IN THE GOOD OLD DAYS
GROUND COVERS FOR EASIER GARDENING
THE CHRISTMAS TREE
LITTLE SAINTS OF CHRISTMAS
GARDEN FLOWERS IN COLOR
VEGETABLE GARDENING IN COLOR
ANNUALS FOR YOUR GARDEN
GARDEN BULBS IN COLOR (co-author)

A Vivid Tapestry of Customs, Traditions, Symbolism, Folklore, History, Legend and Story

CHILTON BOOKS

A DIVISION OF CHILTON COMPANY

Publishers

PHILADELPHIA   NEW YORK

Easter Garland

By
Priscilla Sawyer Lord & Daniel J. Foley

Line Drawings by
CHARLOTTE EDMANDS BOWDEN

Republished by Omnigraphics • Penobscot Building • Detroit • 1999

Copyright © 1963 by
PRISCILLA SAWYER LORD AND DANIEL J. FOLEY

First Edition

Library of Congress Cataloging-in-Publication Data

Lord, Priscilla Sawyer.
    Easter garland / by Priscilla Sawyer Lord & Daniel J. Foley ; line drawings by Charlotte Edmands Bowden.
      p. cm.
    Includes bibliographical references and index.
    ISBN 0-7808-0316-7 (lib. bdg. : alk paper)
    1. Easter.   I. Foley, Daniel J.   II. Title.
GT4935.L6   1999
394.2667 — dc21   99-29132
                                                                                        CIP

This book is printed on acid-free paper meeting the ANSI Z39.48 Standard. The infinity symbol that appears above indicates that the paper in this book meets that standard.

Printed in the United States

For
PHILIP, BEVERLEY, ROBERTA

In Appreciation

Two families who lived in the atmosphere of Easter for more than a year have given us some concept of the true message of Easter—which is Hope.

To Charlotte Edmande Bowden, who interpreted the various chapters with her charming live sketches, and to C. Sally Low, who rendered various woodcuts from old herbals.

To Miss Winnifred Foley for technical assistance.

To countless friends and relatives who shared recipes, traditions, and love and made available those delightful Victorian scrapbooks filled with brightly colored lithographs.

To Dorothy S. Garfield, for typing the manuscript and handling the numerous details relating to the preparation of this book.

To the following individuals and institutions, we are deeply grateful for advice, assistance, and information:

Abbot Public Library
Rev. and Mrs. Charles T. Allen
The American Orchid Society
Miss Katherine T. Bass
Miss Ade Bethune
Mrs. Betty Blaisdell
Mrs. Vera Borkovec
The Boston Athenaeum
Miss Joanne Bridges
Miss Margaret M. Brine
Miss Eleanor Broadhead
Miss Elizabeth Broadhead
Mrs. Sterling Brown
Mr. and Mrs. John A. Burnham, Jr.

Mr. Charles A. Butts
Dr. Timothy J. Clifford
Mrs. Harry Cobb
Mrs. Francis S. Dane
Davison Art Centre, Wesleyan
   Univ., Middletown, Conn.
Mr. Gordon Dillon
Mrs. Pauline Dooley
Mrs. Genevieve M. Elwell
Essex Institute, Salem, Mass.
Mr. Richard Floyd
Forest Lawn Museum
   Glendale, California
Mrs. W. W. K. Freeman

Mrs. William W. Gallagher
Rev. John J. Grant
Rev. Dr. Robert M. Grey
Mrs. W. C. Gungle
Miss Margaret Hackett
Miss Myrta A. Hall
Mrs. Donald Hunt
Mrs. John S. Lancy
Dr. George L. Laverty
Miss Anne A. Lord
Miss Katherine Van Etten Lyford
Mrs. Jeanette McLaughlin
Miss Gertrude E. Mahan
Miss Dorothy S. Manks
Marchal, Inc., New York, N. Y.
The Massachusetts Horticultural Society
Mrs. Joseph L. Miller
National Park Service
New Mexico Magazine
Mrs. Douglas O. Nystedt
Perrini, New York, N. Y.
Mrs. Charles H. Potter
Mrs. Mark A. Princi
Frances Dianne Robotti
Salem Public Library
Mrs. Frank H. Sawyer
Mrs. Dorothy Dean Scott
Swampscott Public Library
Mr. George Taloumis
The Great Masterpiece, Inc.
  Lake Wales, Florida
The National Society for Crippled
  Children and Adults
Mrs. Hanson Hart Webster
Mrs. Thomas D. Welch
Mrs. Samuel A. Whitmore
Woburn Public Library
Yankee Magazine

We are grateful to the following publishers for permission to include the selections indicated:

Century Co., for *The General's Easter Box* by Temple Bailey from *Easter in Modern Story*.

Doubleday Co., Inc., for *Ys and Her Bells* by Marguerite Clement from *Once in France* by Marguerite Clement.

Milton Bradley Co., for *The Sugar Egg* by Carolyn Sherwin Bailey from *Merry Tales for Children*.

E. P. Dutton, for *The Golden Egg* by Ivy Bolton from *Easter Chimes* by Wilhelmina Harper.

Priscilla Sawyer Lord
Daniel J. Foley

Introduction

The story of Easter in all its splendor and glory has been told and retold countless times during the past nineteen hundred years. Matthew, Mark, Luke and John were our earliest chroniclers. As their accounts were passed down by word of mouth from father to son and later recorded on the printed page, they were embellished and enriched by a wealth of folklore and legend, as is the way with men when they tell a story. In like manner, myth and symbol have played a vital part in the narration of Christ's Resurrection.

Thus, the account of the "Feast of the New Life" has been colored and expanded with an abundance of customs and traditions. These have been linked with the observance of the Lenten season over a period of centuries. The manner in which these age-old observances have emerged and been passed down from generation to generation in the folklore of practically every country of the world has added lustre to the significance of the Easter season for all of us. However, many of these customs and traditions have been outmoded and forgotten and others have lost their meaning entirely. In assembling the many facets of this story, we have gathered together the golden threads of history, tradition, and folklore to convey in words the essence of Easter.

To most of us, Easter is more than a day on which we put on the latest in fashion or merely something new and fresh in the way of a garment. In the early days of the Christian Era, the notion of putting on something new was a symbolic act connoting rebirth. Nearly two thousand years have elapsed since the time of our Saviour's Resurrection and the meaning behind this symbolic custom has been largely forgotten. Yet, the significance of symbols which was once so commonplace and so much a part of everyday life has never disappeared entirely. From time to time, down through the ages, symbols have come in sharp focus as men have pursued the true meaning of life. And, strange as it may seem, this age of atomic development has given rise to a new awareness of the symbols by which men have lived for centuries. The observance of Easter and of the entire Lenten season is filled with them and they serve to illustrate the pages of this book.

It is hoped that this volume will provide the reader with a source of information and inspiration about the Easter season which is the beginning of that eternal time when hope springs forth anew in human hearts, the world over.

Contents

	In Appreciation	ix
	Introduction	xi
1 ·	The Message of Easter	1
2 ·	The Meaning of Easter	7
3 ·	The Lore of Easter Plants and Flowers	9
4 ·	Trees of the Cross	23
5 ·	Birds in the Easter Story	29
6 ·	Animals in the Easter Story	37
7 ·	Foods of the Easter Season	45
8 ·	The Easter Egg	67
9 ·	Winter Demons and Mardi Gras	79
10 ·	Forty Days and Easter	83
11 ·	The Holy Grail	93
12 ·	A Seal with a Symbol	97
13 ·	The Glory of the Sun	101
	Stories of Easter:	
	The Sugar Egg, by Carolyn Sherwin Bailey	109
	The Golden Egg, by Ivy Bolton	110
	Ponce de Leon Finds the Land of Flowers, adapted by Woodbury Lowery	115
	A Handful of Clay, by Henry van Dyke	116
	The General's Easter Box, by Temple Bailey	118
	Ys and Her Bells, by Marguerite Clement	122
	Bibliography	129
	Books for Children About Easter	133
	Index	135

Easter Garland

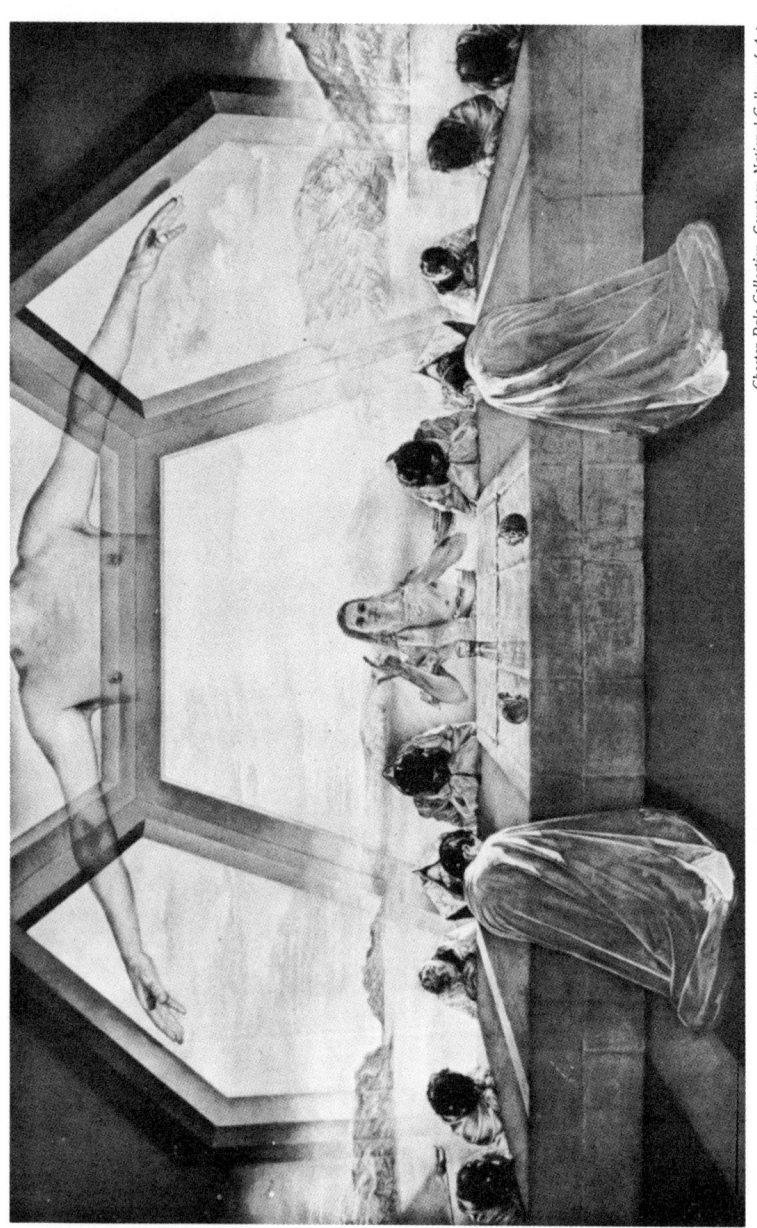

The Sacrament of the Last Supper by Salvador Dali. Chester Dale Collection. Courtesy National Gallery of Art.

1
The Message of Easter

THE LAST SUPPER
According to Matthew 26:17–56

Now the first day of the feast of unleavened bread the disciples came to Jesus, saying unto him, Where wilt thou that we prepare for thee to eat the passover?

And he said, Go into the city to such a man, and say unto him, The Master saith, My time is at hand; I will keep the passover at thy house with my disciples.

And the disciples did as Jesus had appointed them; and they made ready the passover.

Now when the even was come, he sat down with the twelve.

And as they did eat, he said, Verily I say unto you, that one of you shall betray me.

And they were exceeding sorrowful, and began every one of them to say unto him, Lord, is it I?

And he answered and said, He that dippeth his hand with me in the dish, the same shall betray me.

The Son of man goeth as it is written of him: but woe unto that man by whom the Son of man is betrayed! it had been good for that man if he had not been born.

Then Judas, which betrayed him, answered and said, Master, is it I? He said unto him, Thou hast said.

And as they were eating, Jesus took bread, and blessed it, and brake it and gave it to the disciples, and said, Take, eat; this is my body.

And he took the cup, and gave thanks, and gave it to them, saying, Drink ye all of it;

For this is my blood of the new testament, which is shed for many for the remission of sins.

But I say unto you, I will not drink henceforth of this fruit of the vine, until that day when I drink it new with you in my Father's kingdom.

And when they had sung an hymn, they went out into the mount of Olives.

Then saith Jesus unto them, All ye shall be offended because of me this night: for it is written, I will smite the shepherd, and the sheep of the flock shall be scattered abroad.

But after I am risen again, I will go before you into Galilee.

Peter answered and said unto him, Though all men shall be offended because of thee, yet will I never be offended.

Jesus said unto him, Verily I say unto thee, That this night, before the cock crow, thou shalt deny me thrice.

Peter said unto him, Though I should die with thee, yet will I not deny thee. Likewise also said all the disciples.

Then cometh Jesus with them unto a place called Gethsemane, and saith unto the disciples, Sit ye here, while I go and pray yonder.

And he took with him Peter and the two sons of Zebedee, and began to be sorrowful and very heavy.

Then saith he unto them, My soul is exceeding sorrowful, even unto death: tarry ye here, and watch with me.

And he went a little farther, and fell on his face, and prayed, saying, O my Father, if it be possible, let this cup pass from me: nevertheless not as I will, but as thou wilt.

And he cometh unto the disciples, and findeth them asleep, and saith unto Peter, What, could ye not watch with me one hour?

Watch and pray, that ye enter not into temptation: the spirit indeed is willing, but the flesh is weak.

He went away again the second time, and prayed, saying, O my Father, if this cup may not pass away from me, except I drink it, thy will be done.

And he came and found them asleep again: for their eyes were heavy.

And he left them, and went away again, and prayed the third time, saying the same words.

Then cometh he to his disciples, and saith unto them, Sleep on now, and take your rest; behold, the hour is at hand, and the Son of man is betrayed into the hands of sinners.

Rise, let us be going: behold, he is at hand that doth betray me.

And while he yet spake, lo, Judas, one of the twelve, came, and with him a great multitude with swords and staves, from the chief priests and elders of the people.

Now he that betrayed him gave them a sign, saying, Whomsoever I shall kiss, that same is he: hold him fast.

And forthwith he came to Jesus, and said, Hail, master; and kissed him.

And Jesus said unto him, Friend, wherefore art thou come? Then came they, and laid hands on Jesus, and took him.

And, behold, one of them which were with Jesus stretched out his hand, and drew his sword, and struck a servant of the high priest's, and smote off his ear.

Then said Jesus unto him, Put up again thy sword into his place; for all they that take the sword shall perish with the sword.

Thinkest thou that I cannot now pray to my Father, and he shall presently give me more than twelve legions of angels?

But how then shall the scriptures be fulfilled, that thus it must be?

In that same hour said Jesus to the multitudes, Are ye come out as against a thief with swords and staves for to take me? I sat daily with you teaching in the temple, and ye laid no hold on me.

But all this was done, that the scriptures of the prophets might be fulfilled. Then all the disciples forsook him, and fled.

THE DEATH OF JESUS
According to Luke 23:1-46

And the whole multitude of them arose, and led him unto Pilate.

And they began to accuse him, saying, We found this fellow perverting the nation, and forbidding to give tribute to Caesar, saying that he himself is Christ a King.

And Pilate asked him, saying, Art thou the King of the Jews? And he answered him and said, Thou sayest it.

Then said Pilate to the chief priests and to the people, I find no fault in this man.

And they were the more fierce, saying, He stirreth up the people, teaching throughout all Jewry, beginning from Galilee to this place.

When Pilate heard of Galilee, he asked whether the man were a Galilaean.

And as soon as he knew that he belonged unto Herod's jurisdiction, he sent him to Herod, who himself also was at Jerusalem at that time.

And when Herod saw Jesus, he was exceeding glad: for he was desirous to see him of a long season, because he had heard many things of him; and he hoped to have seen some miracle done by him.

Then he questioned with him in many words; but he answered him nothing.

And the chief priests and scribes stood and vehemently accused him.

And Herod with his men of war set him at nought, and mocked him, and arrayed him in a gorgeous robe, and sent him again to Pilate.

And the same day Pilate and Herod were made friends together: for before they were at enmity between themselves.

And Pilate, when he had called together the chief priests and the rulers and the people,

Said unto them, Ye have brought this man unto me, as one that perverteth the people: and, behold, I, having examined him before you, have found no fault in this man touching those things whereof ye accuse him:

No, nor yet Herod: for I sent you to him; and, lo, nothing worthy of death is done unto him.

I will therefore chastise him, and release him.

(For of necessity he must release one unto them at the feast.)

And they cried out all at once, saying, Away with this man, and release unto us Barabbas:

(Who for a certain sedition made in the city, and for murder, was cast into prison.)

Pilate, therefore, willing to release Jesus, spake again to them.

But they cried, saying, Crucify him, crucify him.

And he said unto them the third time, Why, what evil hath he done? I found no cause of death in him: I will therefore chastise him, and let him go.

And they were instant with loud voices, requiring that he might be crucified. And the voices of them and of the chief priests prevailed.

And Pilate gave sentence that it should be as they required.

And he released unto them him that for sedition and murder was cast into prison, who they had desired; but he delivered Jesus to their will.

And as they led him away, they laid hold upon one Simon, a Cyrenian, coming out of the country, and on him they laid the cross, that he might bear it after Jesus.

And there followed him a great company of people, and of women, which also bewailed and lamented him.

But Jesus turning unto them said, Daughters of Jerusalem, weep not for me, but weep for yourselves, and for your children.

For, behold, the days are coming, in the which they shall say, Blessed are the barren, and the wombs that never bare, and the paps which never gave suck.

Then shall they begin to say to the mountains, Fall on us, and to the hills, Cover us.

For if they do these things in a green tree, what shall be done in the dry?

And there were also two other, malefactors, led with him to be put to death.

And when they were come to the place, which is called Calvary, there they crucified him, and the malefactors, one on the right hand, and the other on the left.

Then said Jesus, Father, forgive them; for they know not what they do. And they parted his raiment, and cast lots.

And the people stood beholding. And the rulers also with them derided him, saying, He saved others; let him save himself, if he be Christ, the chosen of God.

And the soldiers also mocked him, coming to him, and offering him vinegar.

And saying, If thou be the king of the Jews, save thyself.

And a superscription also was written over him in letters of Greek, and Latin, and Hebrew, THIS IS THE KING OF THE JEWS.

And one of the malefactors which were hanged railed on him, saying, If thou be Christ, save thyself and us.

But the other answering rebuked him, saying, Dost not thou fear God, seeing thou art in the same condemnation?

And we indeed justly, for we receive the due reward of our deeds: but this man hath done nothing amiss.

And he said unto Jesus, Lord remember me when thou comest into thy kingdom.

And Jesus said unto him, Verily I say unto thee, Today shalt thou be with me in paradise.

And it was about the sixth hour, and there was a darkness over all the earth until the ninth hour.

And the sun was darkened, and the veil of the temple was rent in the midst.

And when Jesus had cried with a loud voice, he said, Father, into thy hands I commend my spirit: and having said thus, he gave up the ghost.

THE RESURRECTION
According to Luke 24:1-31

Now upon the first day of the week, very early in the morning, they came unto the sepulchre, bringing the spices which they had prepared, and certain others with them.

And they found the stone rolled away from the sepulchre.

And they entered in, and found not the body of the Lord Jesus.

And it came to pass, as they were much perplexed thereabout, behold, two men stood by them in shining garments:

And as they were afraid, and bowed down their faces to the earth, they said unto them, Why seek ye the living among the dead?

He is not here, but is risen: remember how He spake unto you when He was yet in Galilee,

Saying, the Son of man must be delivered into the hands of sinful men, and be crucified, and the third day rise again.

And they remembered His words.

And returned from the sepulchre, and told all these things unto the eleven, and to all the rest.

It was Mary Magdalene, and Joanna, and Mary the mother of James, and other women that were with them, which told these things unto the apostles.

And their words seemed to them as idle tales, and they believed them not.

Then arose Peter, and ran unto the sepulchre; and stooping down, he beheld the linen clothes laid by themselves, and departed, wondering in himself at that which was come to pass.

And, behold, two of them went that same day to a village called Emmaus, which was from Jerusalem about threescore furlongs.

And they talked together of all these things which had happened.

And it came to pass, that, while they communed together and reasoned, Jesus Himself drew near, and went with them.

But their eyes were holden that they should not know Him.

And He said unto them, What manner of communications are these that ye have one to another, as ye walk, and are sad?

And the one of them, whose name was Cleopas, answering said unto Him, Art thou only a stranger in Jerusalem, and hast not known the things which are come to pass there in these days?

And He said unto them, What things? And they said unto Him, Concerning Jesus of Nazareth, which was a prophet mighty in deed and word before God and all the people:

And how the chief priests and our rulers delivered Him to be condemned to death, and have crucified Him.

But we trusted that it had been He which should have redeemed Israel: and beside all this, today is the third day since these things were done.

Yea, and certain women also of our company made us astonished, which were early at the sepulchre;

And when they found not His body, they came, saying, that they had also seen a vision of angels, which said that He was alive.

And certain of them which were with us went to the sepulchre, and found it even so as the women had said: but Him they saw not.

Then He said unto them, O fools, and slow of heart to believe all that the prophets have spoken:

Ought not Christ to have suffered these things, and to enter into His glory?

And beginning at Moses and all the prophets, He expounded unto them in all the scriptures the things concerning Himself.

And they drew nigh unto the village, whither they went: and He made as though He would have gone further.

But they constrained Him, saying, Abide with us: for it is toward evening, and the day is far spent. And He went in to tarry with them.

And it came to pass, as He sat at meat with them, He took bread, and blessed it, and brake, and gave to them.

And their eyes were opened, and they knew Him; and He vanished out of their sight.

2
The Meaning of Easter

As we trace the name "Easter" and its roots in the languages of Europe, we learn that it refers to the season of the rising sun, or the dawn. This meaning for Easter long antedates the Christian era, and was adopted as appropriate to designate the Resurrection, the "Feast of the New Life." That illustrious monk and writer of the medieval Church, the Venerable Bede, is often quoted as referring to Easter as being derived from *Eostre,* the name of an Anglo-Saxon goddess, but present-day scholars claim that no such person was known in German mythology.

Also referred to as the "Great Night" and the "Great Day," "The Feast of Feasts," this "Solemnity of Solemnities" is spoken of in Hungary as the "Feast of Meat," indicating that the Lenten fast is over.

Most of the nations of Europe refer to Easter as *Pasch,* a Greek term derived from the Hebrew, meaning "Passover." Christ was crucified on Passover Day. This important feast in the Jewish calendar was observed in thanksgiving for the deliverance of the Israelites the night before they fled from Egypt. The firstborn of each Egyptian family was destroyed by the angel of God, but the children of the Israelites had been spared. Moses, proclaiming the command of God, ordered that each Hebrew family should slay a lamb without blemish and sprinkle its blood on the doorframe of each house. Following this sacrifice, the lamb was roasted and eaten with the traditional unleavened bread, and garnished with bitter herbs. As set down in Jewish law, the ceremony was to take place annually on the eve of the passover, and is still practiced by orthodox Jews. Christ participated in this rite the night before His crucifixion. The sacrificial lamb of the Hebrews became the Christian symbol of Christ, the "Lamb of God, which taketh away the sin of the world," John 1:29.

The variable dates of Easter are sometimes confusing, especially to those who deal in commerce. The possibilities of fixing the date for Easter so that it occurs

 at the same time annually have been discussed on many occasions, but the method of determining Easter has remained unchanged for more than 1600 years. The celebration of the Passover, governed by the moon, had been set according to custom for generations at the time of the birth of Christ. The early Christians, following this ancient practice, declared that Easter should be observed on the first Sunday following the full moon that occurs on or following the spring equinox, near or on March 21. The meeting of the astronomers of Alexandria under the direction of the archbishop of that great city resulted in the Council of Nicea, which set the method of calculating the date of Easter in A.D. 325. Thus, Easter is spoken of as a movable feast which may occur as early as March 22nd or as late as April 25th. During the past fifty years, Easter has been observed four times as often in April as it has in March.

The story of Easter is summed up in the words "hope" and "eternal life." Around this "Feast of Feasts" which commemorates the greatest of miracles, the Resurrection of Christ, have evolved a host of traditions and legends. In ritual, in hymns, in folk customs, it manifests itself in the humblest of everyday practices, from the foods we eat to the new clothes we put on. The outward manifestations of nature mirror in a variety of ways the spirit of hope that wells up in every human heart at Easter. Spring and Easter are synonymous. Symbols reveal themselves in the flowers of the field, the birds of the air, and the familiar animals.

The spirit of Christmas is best expressed in the joy of children who marvel at the birth of the Saviour in an image they understand, for He is like them— a child, yet the King of the World. Easter is somewhat more complex, for the very concept of the risen Christ requires the mental grasp of the growing child old enough to have attained the use of reason. But the message of Easter, when described in the terms of the eternal symphony of spring, becomes the supreme lesson of faith for mankind.

Aside from the Christian concept of Easter and its Hebrew roots, the pre-Christian or pagan myths and folklore that surround this feast of spring have clothed its observance in a world-wide blending of ancient traditions. Down through the ages, the fear and the mystery surrounding death have been no less puzzling than the renewal of life and the rebirth of the spirit. "Except a corn of wheat fall into the ground and die, it abideth alone: but if it die, it bringeth forth much fruit." In these simple words Christ summed up the mysterious truth that life depends on death. John 12:24.

Myth and symbol go hand in hand as historical facts are related and blended with age-old beliefs and customs which attempt to explain eternal truth and historic fact as Christ did in giving the parables to His first followers. In a book which attempts to bring together history, myth, symbols, folklore, and traditions, the aim must be to relate and yet to distinguish the various categories that provide the threads that make the marvelous tapestry of Easter in all its glory, radiance, and richness.

3
The Lore of Easter Plants and Flowers

The plants and the flowers associated with Easter are among the loveliest of the entire growing year. They glow with color, emitting sweet fragrance, and convey the eternal message of hope when given as presents. But there are some that are associated with the passion of our Saviour, reminding us of the cruelty of nature concealed in protective thorns and spines and the uses to which man has put them in bestowing punishment.

With many plants associated with the Holy Family, legends and traditions have literally sprung from the earth in various parts of the world down through the ages, due in part to the similarity or relationship or resemblance of some local plant to one found in the Holy Land. Moreover, when looked upon as symbols of memorable events or simple reminders of faith, they serve to convey the message intended. One of the common briers with showy red blossoms (*Rubus coronaricus*) is believed to have derived its red color from the Saviour's blood. An ancient German tradition has it that the glossy-leaved holly commonly called English holly (*Ilex aquifolium*) had its white fruits changed to red in a similar manner. There is a white-fruited form of holly grown in gardens, but it is not common—it is merely a variant or an albino form, a condition which often occurs in the plant world. Yet, the facts do little to discount the folk belief, which is usually colorful and easy to remember.

Was the crown of thorns, that was plaited by the soldiers and placed on Christ's head in mockery, actually a wreath of rose canes, as implied by some of the great Renaissance painters? No other flower that grows in gardens or in the

 wild is richer in lore than the rose. This emblem of love, beauty, and youth can be traced back five thousand years or more, and its associations with the Holy Family are numerous. It is often referred to as the flower of the martyrs. The name "rose" has been used for many plants that are not true roses or related to the rose family. The term Rose of Sharon has been applied to a wild tulip and a handsome flowering shrub which blooms in summer (*Hibiscus syriacus*). Other plants referred to as roses are the oleander, the crocus, and the narcissus. In many parts of Europe, the wild rose is referred to in folklore as the plant used in Christ's passion. The flowers were originally white, but changed color, having been dyed with the blood of the Saviour as the crown rested on His brow. There are several kinds of wild roses native to Palestine, and Bible scholars have written voluminously about the word "rose" as used in the Bible.

In Germany, France, and Great Britain, tradition has it that the white hawthorn (*Crataegus oxyacantha*), familiar shrub of English hedgerows and gardens, was the plant used. Other plants mentioned are the box thorn (*Lycium europaeum*), the wild hyssop (*Capavris spinosa*), and the bramble (*Rubus fruticosus*). The common barberry (*Berberis vulgaris*) is pointed out in Italy as the source of the crown.

Of all the plants mentioned as the source of the torturing crown, none is better known than the hawthorn. So abundant are its white blossoms in spring that its long, spiny thorns are hardly noticeable, but they are capable of inflicting a painful wound and their sharpness is soon apparent when branches are carelessly handled. An age-old tale recalls that on the way to Calvary a bird fluttered down to the head of the weary Christ and pulled out a thorn that was piercing His brow. The sacred blood colored the breast feathers of the little creature, who has worn the mark since that day, and we know him as robin red-breast.

In England, hawthorn often blooms during mild periods in winter, and the famous Glastonbury Thorn has frequently put forth flowers at Christmas. According to tradition, this holy thorn was brought to England in the first century by Joseph of Arimathea, when he settled there and taught Christianity to the Britons. He had been banished from the Holy Land after the Resurrection. On reaching Wearyall Hill, near Glastonbury, he struck his walking staff into the earth to indicate the location of his new home. Leaving it thus in the soil, the sap stirred to fresh life, put forth leaves, and flourished for centuries as a revered tree. It was finally destroyed by the Puritans as a Romish superstition, but scions were perpetuated and one planted from the original tree on the grounds of the National Cathedral in Washington, D.C., has bloomed on five occasions since 1918.

The fabled hawthorn is truly rich in Scriptural tradition. A little-known story reveals that, while Christ was resting in a grove during His most perilous hours, the magpies covered Him with hawthorn boughs, which the swallows, "fowls of God," removed as soon as His enemies had passed. From this episode the plant gained holiness. A tale concerning Charlemagne related that he knelt before the crown of thorns in the church of Sainte Chapelle in Paris, which was believed to have been made of hawthorn. He was overcome when the wood, dry for centuries, burst into bloom and the air was filled with a wondrous fragrance.

The crown of thorns (*Euphorbia splendens*), a familiar house plant in cold climates noted for its bright vermilion flowers, is probably the plant most frequently associated in the popular mind with Christ. Its woody stems are heavily set with the sharpest of spines of various sizes, making it exceedingly difficult to handle. Yet this woody vine-like shrub, native to Madagascar, was unknown in Bible times.

An acacia, known to the Israelites as the Shittah-tree, is referred to in the Near East as the source of the crown of thorns. It was chosen, sacred tree that it was, because the leaves between the thorns resembled those of ivy, with which kings and princes and great heroes were crowned. No form of mockery could have been more subtle, for the wood of the acacia was considered sacred by the Hebrews. They had brought the acacia out of Egypt and used the wood to build both their Tabernacle and the Ark of the Covenant.

In parts of the Orient a plant called butcher's broom, or prickly-rush (*Ruscus aculeatus*) is believed to be the plant used in the mock coronation. This plant, grown commercially on the West Coast of the United States and known as ruscus, is dried, dyed red and used in Christmas decorations. Visitors to the West Indies are shown the cashew (*Anacardium occidentale*), and told that it was used to make Christ's painful crown.

One old legend not commonly heard concerns the willow. Its branches were used to make the ignoble wreath since this plant originally had thorns. However, the tree wept and drooped at having caused the Saviour so much pain, and the sharp thorns changed themselves into soft, sad-colored leaves that they might never cause any more suffering.

The Christ thorn (*Paliurus spina-cristi*), a plant with thin pliable twigs and fiercely sharp spines found abundantly in Palestine, has received its common name from its supposed use. This plant is believed to be the source of the "wreath of thorny twigs" that was placed on Christ's head as he stood in a scarlet cloak.

One noted scholar maintains that the plant actually used was the spiny burnet (*Poterium spinosum*), a tangled shrub with curious reddish flowers and delicately cut leaves which disappear in the heat of summer. Commonly used as fuel for lime-kilns and ovens, it is gathered and cut with pruning hooks. It burns, making a noisy crackling spitting sound, and is the plant referred to in Ecclesiastes 7:6, "For as the crackling of thorns under a pot, so is the laughter of the fool . . ."

The true lily of the field (*Anemone coronaria*) or wind flower, a superb wild flower of Palestine widely cultivated in greenhouses and gardens today, appears in many colors, including white, purple, pink, and red. It is traditionally associated with the passion of Christ. It is claimed that those with red flowers owe

their color to the drops of blood which fell on the flowers as Christ hung on the cross.

At the time of the Crusades, Umberto, Bishop of Pisa, suggested that ships returning from the Holy Land should bring back good soil, instead of sand, for ballast. The sacred earth so obtained was spread on the ground of Campo Santo and Pisa and the marvelous wind flower appeared there, where it is now naturalized.

Another favorite flower, the lily-of-the-valley, is said to have sprung from the tears of Mary, the mother of Jesus, as she wept at the foot of the cross, yet this flower is unknown in the Holy Land. But it is beautiful in form, pure white, as precious as any jewel, and in the language of myth and legend serves as a kind of parable. Flowering plants have been a never-ending source of joy to poets, painters, and peasants down through the ages: they speak the language of the heart.

A wild verbena known as American blue vervain (*Verbena hastata*), which resembles a species found in Brittany, is known as the "herb of the cross," for it is said to have been found at the foot of the cross.

Selma Lagerlöf, noted Swedish writer of stories and legends, has produced a memorable story, entitled "St. Veronica's Handkerchief." In it she recounts in great detail a moving incident of Jesus on His way to Calvary. As He was passing the home of a humble woman, He sank to the ground under the weight of the heavy cross He was carrying. She gave Him her veil to wipe His brow, and it is said, according to early Roman Catholic tradition, that the Saviour's image was imprinted on the cloth. From the sweat that fell to the ground there sprouted a blue-flowering plant in which a tiny image appears in each dainty bloom, arranged along a slender stem. The flower was called veronica in tribute to the woman who befriended Jesus.

A curious plant found in Jericho, Syria, and the Mediterranean which botanists refer to as the Palestine tumbleweed is popularly known as the resurrection plant (*Anastatica hierochuntica*). To the Jewish people it is the Rose of Jericho. In the Old World it is known as Rosa-Mariae, the Rose of the Virgin, or Mary's hand. Yet, it in no way resembles a rose. The Moslems call it Kaf Marjam, and to all it has been a cherished plant for centuries. According to legend, it sprang up wherever the Holy Family rested on the flight into Egypt. It is said to have blossomed at the Saviour's birth, closed at the crucifixion, and opened again at Easter; thus the name resurrection flower. When withered, the plant rolls up like a ball, but it resumes its natural form whenever it is placed in water or exposed to dampness. It is sometimes offered in novelty shops as a curiosity, and from time to time has been featured by street peddlers and hawkers of strange merchandise. In Psalm 83:13 we find this passage: "O my God, make them like a wheel; as the stubble before the wind"—a reference to the resurrection plant.

The crown imperial, or fritillary, is a curious plant with bulb-like roots, sometimes grown in gardens, and native to Persia. The bell-like flowers, which are usually red or yellow, were originally white. According to an old German legend, this flower failed to bow in the Garden of Gethsemane during the agony of the Saviour, and since that time it has hung its head, blushing red with shame, and with tears of repentance in its eyes. The tears are drops of standing sweet dew in the white centers of the blossoms.

The showy reddish fruit of the pomegranate is a symbol of the Resurrection often found in Christian art, including painting, sculpture, and embroidery. This plant is linked with Proserpine, daughter of Ceres, goddess of the earth, who was kidnaped by Pluto. She finally returned to her mother, but because she had eaten six pomegranate seeds, she had to remain with Pluto for six months each year, in his underground kingdom. This old Roman legend was transferred to Christian tradition to signify that the Lord had power to burst forth from the tomb and live again.

On the night of the crucifixion, we read in John 19:39, 40 that Nicodemus came "and brought a mixture of myrrh and aloes, about an hundred pound weight. Then took they the body of Jesus, and wound it in linen clothes with the spices, as the manner of the Jews is to bury." Myrrh is derived from a thorny bush in the form of a gum resin which comes from the branches. It is an astringent and cleansing agent used by the ancient Hebrews and other races in embalming. Since it was not found in Palestine, it had to be imported from Arabia or Africa in Bible times. Aloe is a plant with stiff succulent leaves, not unlike the century plant in appearance, with spikes of showy red flowers. Like the century plant which grows in our American deserts, it grows in hot, dry places, but was not native to Palestine and was also imported from Africa. In Jesus' time this drug was used in embalming and was considered costly.

A legend beloved by children relating to Jesus concerns the larkspur. It relates to the Garden of Gethsemane, where Jesus loved to walk. There the grass was greener, the sky bluer, and the sun brighter than anywhere else; there colorful flowers bloomed and little animals lived. For a while Jesus did not come to the garden. All His little friends missed Him, and particularly a small rabbit, who waited day and night for the return of the Master. Early on the third day Christ came—and as He walked into the sunshine He gave the rabbit a loving smile. Later, when Jesus' friends came to the garden to pray, they found a path of beautiful flowers—the larkspurs. To this day one may see in the center of each blossom an image of the little rabbit who waited three days and three nights to greet the risen Lord.

Familiar to many as a handsome winter house plant and to gardeners as an alpine gem in the autumn garden, cyclamen is a common wild flower in the Holy Land. The Roman Catholics long ago dedicated it to the Virgin Mary because the sword of sorrow that pierced her heart at the time of the crucifixion is symbolized in the drop of blood in the heart of the flower.

Lent lily, wild daffodil, daffy-down-dilly, Easter lily, Easter rose, golden

trumpets—these and a score or more of colorful local names are applied to the common wild daffodil or narcissus found native in England. Poets and garden writers have extolled the virtues and the beauty of this trumpet flower, which is nature's cloth of gold. A. E. Housman has given us a memorable picture in his poem, "The Lent Lily":

> " 'Tis spring; come out to ramble
> The hilly brakes around,
> For under thorn and bramble
> About the hollow ground
> The primroses are found.
>
> "And there's the windflower chilly
> With all the winds at play,
> And there's the Lenten lily
> That has not long to stay
> And dies on Easter day.
>
> "And since till girls go maying
> You find the primrose still,
> And find the windflower playing
> With every wind at will,
> But not the daffodil,
>
> "Bring baskets now, and sally
> Upon the spring's array,
> And bear from hill and valley
> The daffodil away
> That dies on Easter day."

Whenever we see it, a few blooms in a pot in a sunny window or planted in drifts in a garden, this is one of the best loved flowers of spring. Some species are native to the Holy Land, and it blooms in many parts of the world during the Lenten season. It is one of the flowers referred to as the lilies of the field.

Of all the plants associated with the crucifixion, perhaps no other blossom can be considered more symbolic than the passion flower. Strangely enough, this plant was unknown in Christ's time. There are more than three hundred kinds native to the tropical areas of America, a few in Asia, and one in Madagascar. An old Spanish legend has it that the passion flower climbed the cross by means of its tendrils and fastened itself about the scars in the wood where the nails had been driven through the hands and feet of the Saviour. Dr. Harold N. Moldenke, author of *Plants of the Bible,* the most complete and authentic book of its kind, has recorded the origin of the legend and obvious symbolism of this remarkable flowering vine.

"In 1610 a Mexican Augustinian friar, Emanuel de Villegas, brought a drawing of a passion-flower (*Passiflora*) to Jacomo Bosio, who was then preparing a work on the cross of Calvary. Here was born the legend of this flower's connection with Jesus. Its bud was taken to be symbolic of the Eucharist; the half-opened flower suggested the Star of the East that guided the Wise Men. The normally 10 sepals and petals were regarded as representing the ten apostles present at the Crucifixion (Peter and Judas being absent). The corona, which is usually present as an outgrowth of the receptacle inwardly from the corolla, was symbolic of the crown of thorns placed on Jesus' head. The usually five stamens suggest the five wounds inflicted in Jesus' body on the cross. The three central styles, with their capitate stigmas, represent the nails used to fasten Him to the cross. In species with only three stamens, these are regarded as representing the hammers used to drive in the nails. The long, axillary, coiling tendrils are symbolic of the cord-like strands of the scourges used to beat Him. The often digitately lobed leaves represent the hands of His persecutors.

"In some species the corona is tinged with red, representing to some the bloody thorns of the crown, to others the bloody scourges. In some species there are five red spots, suggesting blood from the five wounds; in other species there are said to be 72 filamentous divisions of the corona, suggesting the 72 thorns said by tradition to have pierced Jesus' brow. In some species the leaves are shaped like the head of a lance or pike, symbolic of the spear used to pierce His side; other species have the lower leaf-surface marked with round silver spots, suggesting the 30 pieces of silver for which He was betrayed."

Numerous wayside plants and wildings have bespoken the passion to peasants and landed gentry alike. In Cheshire there is found a wild orchid (*Orchis maculata*), that is known locally as Gethsemane, for the spots of the flowers are believed to have resulted from drops of bloody sweat that fell from Christ's brow in the Garden of Gethsemane.

Another orchid native to South America has a charming association with Easter, since it is commonly referred to as the Easter orchid. When orchid culture first captivated Europe more than a century ago, a young French botanist named Pierre de Vert was sent to French Guiana by a Paris nobleman to secure the most beautiful wild orchid available for the Easter Festival. The botanist was given one of the coveted gold medals awarded at the Vatican, which was valued at 500 francs and would serve as an aid in returning him to France if his money gave out. Charles M. Skinner has related this tale in *Myths and Legends Beyond Our Borders*.

"Landing in Cayenne, Pierre set off at once for Mount Roraima, of which fabulous tales had reached his ears, and, careless of malaria, of tormenting insects, of wild beasts, of loathsome snakes, he reached the highlands where he hoped to find the largest and most striking of the orchids. During his search he stumbled on the habitations of a rude hill tribe of savages. They were unable to understand why he had come among them; they had suffered from the treachery and misconduct of the whites; they disbelieved him when he said

that he had travelled all the way from the farther shore of the great water to seek flowers, because flowers could be had in any place: so they took him prisoner, and the unrestrained clamored to have him roasted. They searched his pockets and took his money. They had seen enough of white men to know how many vices could be indulged with gold. 'Is this all?' asked the chief, holding the coins before him.

"Pierre was about to answer, 'Yes,' but as he placed his hand on his heart he felt the medal there. He could not lie.

" 'All?' repeated the Indian.

"Pierre bit his lip and looked into the sky. It was hard to be robbed of every coin, and have to give up his medal also.

"Pierre shook his head, parted his clothing at the throat, and revealed the medal.

" 'The lad will not lie, yet he is white!' exclaimed one of his captors, in astonishment.

" 'It is his soul that is white,' declared another.

"The people would not touch the medal. Pierre had won them. They made a bed of fragrant leaves for him, and he slept unguarded until the call of birds aroused him in the morning. When the Indians had shared their meal with him, they gave back the money they had taken. 'You are good,' they said. 'You do not deceive. Keep your coins and rest, and we will help you.'

"The people dispersed, and did not return until night. When they came back, they were laden with the strangest and most exquisite blossoms, whose heavy perfume was almost overpowering. One of these was of remarkable size and color, and that one, Pierre knew, would win the prize. He detached the plant from the tree to which it had fastened, and some weeks afterward it bloomed in Notre Dame. The wonder and admiration of the people were almost reward enough for his toil and hardship. With the money he received as a prize he returned to Guiana and taught the gospel to the Indians."

The dove orchid, or Holy Ghost plant, considered one of the most astonishing examples of mimicry and symbolism in the orchid family, is native to Panama, where it is referred to as "el Espirito Santo." The white wax-like blossoms which appear in summer measure three inches across, are delightfully fragrant, and last for weeks when cut. Like the early Christians who were deeply aware of symbols and saw the handiwork of the Saviour everywhere, particularly in nature, the natives of Panama venerate this beautiful orchid which they believe has mystical qualities, because of its close resemblance to a dove. Unfortunately, this orchid has become exceedingly rare in the wild, because of the careless exploitation of curiosity seekers who gather the blooms and destroy the plants by improper handling.

Margaret Thornington Preston has given us the significance of this extraordinary orchid in her poem, "Flower of the Holy Spirit."

"Espirito Santo, flower of the jungle,
  Message of mystical light;
Born in mysterious gloom,
  Breath of an Infinite Might;
Sweet benediction, dove in a blossom,
  Poised in a chalice of white,
Prayerfully bending thy head,
  Spreading thy wings as for flight.

"Panama's orchid, sign of the Spirit,
  Flower with a bird in thy heart;
Rarest of tropical bloom,
  Symbol of wonder thou art.
Traceried sunlight sifts through the woven
  Roof of the jungle, to guide
Natives in searching for thee,
  Lighting their way to thy side.

"Miracle blossom, clad in thy waxen
  Raiment, surpassing the King's:
Taking no thought, yet behold!
  Flower of the Spirit, with wings.
Radiant Passion flowers, flashing around thee,
  Seem to be flouting thy sign;
Dove of the mystical realm,
  What is thy message divine?"

The folklore of plants in the Old World is widely known, but we are inclined to overlook the tropical areas of the world, whence came the passion flowers and the Holy Ghost plant. M. A. Purdan, noted orchid enthusiast, painted a vivid picture of Easter in the jungle in an article which he wrote for the *American Orchid Society Bulletin* more than twenty years ago.

"Does the jungle know it is Lent? Every day of every year, the jungle has blooming orchids tucked somewhere among its green frills. Just now the jungle may be likened unto a great cathedral with trees as columns upholding the ceiling which is decorated by the Maker of orchids. In fact the jungle is keeping Lent and making ready for Holy Week by preparing thousands of purple orchid blossoms. Locally these highly perfumed blossoms are called 'Semana Santa,' being in full bloom at this time.

"In remote regions where humble folk know not their city kin, this orchid is now much in evidence. It sings a purple harmony of love and faith by its beautiful presence at every little wooden cross at the roadside. The pretentious shrines have their blossoms in eastern ollas of cool water so the blossoms endure

several weeks. Church altars are purple with these orchids. The patron saint of every mountain home is beflowered, purple and sweet.

". . . The entire plant is attractive—a fragrant cluster of bright blossoms on a long, slender stalk, a bunch of fat, green and bronze bulbs ending in long, green leaves. Each precious blossom has six petals, five are long, slender, curving backward then forward and are usually brownish purple. The ornamental sixth petal which always hangs down is large, heart-shaped with edges a bit ruffled. The color may be pale mauve with crimson lines where the white column peeps out, or it may be the deepest, richest purple of the color pots of Persia.

"And the perfume? It is such a mystery. Yesterday the little girl, Libby Lundy, dissected this blossom, making a botanical sketch. Long after the petals had been severed, the child marveled each petal exhaled its innate perfume bringing to mind: 'sweet mystery of life if I could know thee'—

"The scientists of the orchid world speak of this orchid as 'Epidendrum atropurpureum,' but we who know it intimately like to say 'Semana Santa'—it ripples over the tongue like music—it really is a short Gregorian chant without an amen, for it never ceases but blows or scatters on and on over the coastal and interior low lands of Panama."

The tulip has its place in Christian lore as one of the flowers referred to as a lily of the field. Several wild tulips are native to Palestine and make the landscape gay when they flower, along with the wild hyacinths, the narcissus, the anemones, and other spring-flowering bulbs. The tulip of Bible literature is not unlike the showy species tulips found in present-day gardens. As a symbol of love and hope at Easter time, the tulip is charmingly portrayed in an old English legend.

In medieval Devon lived an old, impoverished woman who wanted no more of life than to contribute some beauty to the spot upon which her small, neat hovel nestled itself. Coupled with this desire was her earnest hope that children would love her. Not far from her modest home was a mansion owned by a man of great wealth who had a garden filled with new and enormously expensive tulips. As the peasant woman passed this spectacular garden on her way to the village, she so yearned for one of these beautiful blooms for her own dooryard that she spent many an hour devising a scheme by which she might afford one.

Known as a maker of tasty cheese, she made an especially large mold of it, and, taking it to the great house where the tulips grew, she asked to see the owner. She requested that he taste her cheese and, although reluctant to do so at first, the gentleman finally sampled it and pronounced it the best he had ever eaten. For her cheese she asked, in exchange, one of his precious tulip bulbs. The next year when the tulip bloomed she watched it with excitement the whole day long. When the chill of the spring evening drove her indoors, she peered out into the dusk at her prize possession and was amazed to see a small baby snuggled into the folds of the closing tulip. It had been placed there by a fairy. Now children would come to call on her, for she had a wondrous story to tell.

In the days that followed she made many a cheese and earned many a tulip from the gentleman in the great house. Her small plot of land became an attraction to children and grown-ups alike. The few years that remained to her were filled with beauty and hope and the wonderment of spring and Christ's remembrance of her. When she died, her humble house was sold to a man who was greedy and insensitive. When the tulips bloomed, he dug them up and threw them into a dump nearby. But, to this day, if you drive by you will find the approach to the dump attractive at Easter time with the blooms of tulips, which cradle the love of children and the hope of a better dwelling place.

Easter Greetings is the name attached to a superb bright pink variety of the Martha Washington geranium, since it is usually brought into bloom by florists for the Easter season. One of the most striking forms of cactus carries the common name of Easter-lily cactus. This native of Brazil is found abundantly in our western desert and when the spring rains come, it bursts forth in all its glory, like a gorgeous Easter lily.

Modesty and innocence are attributes of the violet, which for centuries has been the object of attention of monarchs, scholars, poets, and common folk. Flower of the wayside and denizen of gardens, it is beloved for its color, its form, and its fragrance. Like many another blossom, it has a legend that links it with the Easter tradition. When the risen Saviour was walking in a grove on Easter morning, each flower lifted its head to see Him. The violet sighed, for being short of stature and partly concealed by luxuriant foliage, it feared that it would remain unnoticed. However, Christ tarried a while to admire this modest purple blossom. Ever after the violet has bowed its face toward the sod in remembrance of that meeting "with the blessed Son of God."

The violet was Napoleon's favorite flower. When he was banished to the Island of Elba, it is said that his friends wore violets to show their loyalty, for they believed that he would return when the violets bloomed again. And he did, in late March, 1815. He made his way to the Tuileries, the royal palace in Paris, France, amid a shower of fragrant purple violets. The Empress Josephine was a great champion of gardening, and set the vogue for violets in France, England, and America which lasted for nearly a hundred years.

Visitors to the Isabel Stewart Gardner Museum in Boston have vivid memories of a silver vase filled with violets which rests on a small table beneath a portrait of Christ, attributed to Giorgione, late fifteenth-century Italian painter. When Mrs. Gardner hung the portrait, it was her wish that fresh violets, symbolic color of Christ's passion, be kept there whenever the picture was viewed. Since violets are not available at all seasons of the year, the blossoms of browallia are substituted from time to time.

The lily lost her rank in Gethsemane when Christ walked there the night before His death. Each and every other flower bent its head in sorrow as He

passed. Yet the lily, shining in the darkness, said, "I am so much fairer than my sisters that I will stand erect on my stalk and gaze at Him as He goes by, in order that He may have the comfort of my loveliness and fragrance." As He saw the flower, He paused before it for a moment, possibly to admire, but as His eye fell upon it in the moonlight, the lily, contrasting her self-satisfaction with his humility, and seeing that all other flowers had bent before Him, was overcome with shame, and the red flush that spread over her face tinges it still. It is called the red lily for that reason, and it never holds its head erect as it did before that night.

Like the Christmas poinsettia, the Easter lily has become the American floral symbol of the greatest festival in the Christian calendar. Yet, both flowers are comparative newcomers in comparison with the age-old feasts which we commemorate. The white lily that has been used by painters and sculptors in religious art for centuries to symbolize purity and innocence, and often seen in gardens, is known as the Madonna lily. It blooms in early summer, but is not easily forced by florists. Thus, the introduction of the Easter lily less than a century ago was a welcome addition to the then small number of white flowers which could be used at Easter. The fact that it was white and fragrant and a true lily made it all the more acceptable.

In the 1880's, Mrs. Thomas P. Sargent, an enthusiastic amateur gardener of Philadelphia, made a trip to Bermuda where she saw gardens filled with white trumpet lilies, known locally as Bermuda lilies. She was so greatly impressed with the fragrance and the beauty of this white lily that she arranged to bring bulbs back to Philadelphia. They soon came to the attention of William K. Harris, a local nurseryman who introduced them to the florist trade under the name of *Lilium Harrisi*. Shortly thereafter, they were featured at spring flower shows in various parts of the country. Ten years later, sizable shipments of bulbs were being made to the United States and England from Bermuda, and a lively trade developed. It was not long before the famous Bermuda lily became known as the Easter lily all over America. The new lily had great appeal for indoor decoration and for use in churches as well, because it could be forced easily for the Easter season.

The story of its introduction is not uncommon in the history of plant lore. More than one hundred years ago, a vessel in distress was forced to anchor in the old Bermuda town of St. George's. Among the passengers was a missionary returning from Japan who happened to be a friend of the Episcopal rector of Hamilton parish. The missionary was also a botanist and had brought home a collection of seeds, plants, and bulbs. Among the bulbs were those of a white lily, found native in a group of islands south of Japan. It was known to the natives as the blunderbuss or gun lily. He presented some of them to the Reverend Mr. Roberts and to the local postmaster. In no time, the bulbs multiplied rapidly under the ideal growing conditions of Bermuda, and were soon widely planted in various parts of the island.

Visitors to Bermuda never fail to marvel at the extensive plantings which are seen there at this time of year. In bygone days, quantities of flowers were shipped to the United States for sale, and those remaining were used to make perfume. When a blight attacked the Easter lilies in Bermuda, efforts were made to grow them in the United States. As a result, the Croft lily, named for Sidney Croft of Bandon, Oregon, was introduced in 1931. Several growers in the Pacific Northwest and in California now produce the majority of bulbs, forced by the million each year for Easter.

"A lesson in each flower,
A story in each tree and bower,
In every herb on which we tread
Are written words, which, rightly read,
Will lead us from earth's fragrant sod
To hope, and holiness to God."

Christ Bearing the Cross by Giorgione.

Courtesy Isabella Stewart Gardner

4
Trees of the Cross

In the Garden of Eden there were many trees, two of which stand out in religion, history, and literature. These are the tree of life and the tree of knowledge of good and evil. "And out of the ground made the Lord God to grow every tree that is pleasant to the sight, and good for food; the tree of life also in the midst of the garden, and the tree of knowledge of good and evil" (Genesis 2:9). The tree of life symbolized the source of sustenance for man to meet his physical and spiritual needs as long as he remained obedient. On the other hand, the fruit-bearing tree of knowledge of good and evil was a symbol to determine the worth of Adam and Eve.

The tree of life in Christian symbolism is exemplified in the cross and its appearance in the Garden of Eden, as pictured to us both in the words of Holy Scripture and in old prints and paintings, may be described or defined as a prefiguration of it. What kind of tree it was has been discussed by scientists and theologians for centuries. It may have been a date palm, a banana, a fig, or a mountain ash. But its physical aspect and the species or kind is of little importance. Essentially it is a symbol, a very ancient one.

The tree of knowledge of good and evil is traditionally referred to as an apple tree, or more correctly as an apricot. Some claim that it was actually a fig tree since Adam and Eve used fig leaves to clothe themselves after eating the forbidden fruit. Others mention it as a palm, a citron, or a pomegranate. Pursuing this tradition further, we learn from several accounts of the origin of the tree of Adam which eventually produced the wood for the cross, the symbol of symbols in the Christian world.

Trees associated with the Resurrection include those which may have furnished the wood of the cross, those used for the scourging, and the palm and the olive, which figured in Christ's triumphal entry into Jerusalem. Then, too, the tree on which Judas hanged himself has also been a subject of great interest down through the ages.

Whence came the wood from which the cross was made has been the source of many fanciful stories. Was it a cedar, a juniper, an oak, an aspen, a pear, a pine, an olive, or an elder? Some of these trees seem more logical choices for speculation than others, because they are native to the Holy Land; others are definite developments of folk tradition. As might be expected, the tree of life from the Garden of Eden has its place in the story, and so, too, does the cedar of Lebanon, one of the mighty and magnificent old trees of Bible times.

An account that appears frequently in ancient writings states that the cross was made of cedar, cypress, and olive wood. Early writers who recorded traditions look back to the Garden of Eden and the story of Seth. When Adam was dying, Seth, his third son, procured a slip or three seeds (according to another account) from the angel guarding the Garden, which he planted in Adam's mouth. From this ceremonial planting sprang a three-branched tree. One branch was of cedar, one of cypress, and the third of olive. This fabulous story relates that David wept for his sins beneath this tree. King Solomon, wishing to destroy the tree, had it cut down, but the wood was too hard to be fashioned for any useful purpose, and was discarded in a swamp. When the Queen of Sheba paid a visit to King Solomon, she was asked to use it as a bridge, but refused. She it was who claimed that she could not walk on the tree that would one day be used to make the cross for the crucifixion of Christ.

During a great storm, an angel took refuge under an ancient cedar. When the weather cleared, he prayed that this noble tree whose fragrant branches had sheltered him might one day bear a fruit of value to the human race. His prayer was answered, since the cedar became the wood of the cross.

The cedar of Lebanon is an impressive evergreen which grows almost exclusively on the Mountain of Lebanon. Great stands of this tree are still to be found there in groves. The twelve oldest and largest are revered by Hebrews, Christians, and Mohammedans alike. To the Israelites, they are the Twelve Friends of Solomon, because the Temple of Solomon was built of cedar wood. To Christians, these trees symbolize the twelve Apostles. Among the Mohammedans, the cedars are looked upon as saints, and it is their belief that evil will overtake anyone who injures one of these trees. Each year at the Feast of the Transfiguration, Armenians, Greeks, and Mormons make a pilgrimage to the Cedars of Lebanon.

When Mary and Joseph were fleeing into Egypt with the Child Jesus, it is claimed that the juniper which we call red cedar (*Juniperus communis*) sheltered the Holy Family from a band of brigands they saw on the road. This same tree has been pointed out as having furnished the wood of the cross.

In Bible times, a garden was usually an orchard where olive trees, figs, and other kinds of fruit were grown. These trees provided welcome shade in the heat of the day. The olive tree grows more picturesque as it attains age, and many have been known to live for hundreds of years. Valued for its fruit, oil, and lumber, the branches of this tree bespeak peace as words cannot. No other tree is more characteristic of the Holy Land or has been more intimately associated with the history of man and the development of civilization than the olive. Many ancient specimens are to be found on the Mount of Olives and at Gethsemane. This tree, steeped in history and mythology, is among those mentioned as having provided the wood from which the cross was made.

The sturdy pine also fits into this colorful tapestry. The cone, when cut lengthwise, displays the form of a hand—the hand of the Saviour. On the flight into Egypt, the Holy Family was concealed beneath a pine, and the tree lowered its limbs as protection from Herod's soldiers. The Child raised His hand in blessing—hence the sign in the fruit. Yet, like the juniper, it too, according to Pomeranian (Prussian) tradition, provided the wood for the cross, with the result that the tree bears the sign of the cross in the structure of its branches.

From Polish tradition comes the account of the aspen or poplar (*Populus tremula*) as the tree of the cross. When the executioners were driving the nails into the wood and the sacred blood was gushing forth, the aspens all over the world began to tremble, and have done so ever since. In another form, the story relates to the fact that Jesus Himself was forced to make His cross of aspen wood. Consequently, the poplar is considered sacred in some lands.

Turning to the Christian lore of Greece, we discover that all the forest trees revolted at the idea of being selected to provide the cross, except the holm oak (*Quercus ilex*). But Jesus pardoned the tree because it accepted death with Him. It was under the shade of a holm oak that He appeared to the Apostles after His Resurrection. Ever since, the tree has lifted its branches to heaven as if praying, and in the Middle Ages it became the tree sacred to Mary, the mother of Jesus.

Curiously enough, there are many legends in Germany about the pear tree relating to Christ. One relates that this tree provided the wood of the cross, and as a result the wood later developed roots and produced red flowers and fruit and leaves similarly veined.

Mistletoe, sacred to the Druids, and traditionally used in Christmas decorations, was originally a tree. An old English belief has it that it furnished its wood for the cross, and as a result was transformed into a parasitic vine, a true pest in areas where it is native. Another vine much cherished in gardens, the showy clematis, was once a tree, according to old Italian tradition. For the ignoble use to which it was put it was transformed into a sprawling vine which must forever scramble in the underbrush.

The alder and the elder (*Sambucus nigra*), found in moist soil, have also been mentioned in this respect. The four quarters of the globe are represented in trees

believed to have been indigenous to their respective areas—the cedar, the cypress, the palm, and the olive—according to the source from which the account was taken.

The best known tree legend in America relating to the cross is the story of the symbolism of our native Eastern dogwood, one of the best loved of flowering trees in parks and gardens. Obviously, since the tree was unknown in Bible lands, it serves as another example of the appeal of myths to explain conspicuous markings on flowers and fruits. At the time of the crucifixion, the dogwood had been the size of the oak and other forest trees. So firm and strong was the tree that it was chosen as the timber for the cross. To be used thus for such a cruel purpose greatly distressed the tree, and Jesus, nailed upon it, sensed this, and in His gentle pity for all sorrow and suffering said to it:

"Because of your regret and pity for My suffering, never again shall the dogwood tree grow large enough to be used as a cross. Henceforth it shall be slender and bent and twisted and its blossoms shall be in the form of a cross . . . two long and two short petals. And in the center of the outer edge of each petal there will be nail prints, brown with rust and stained with red, and in the center of the flower will be a crown of thorns, and all who see it will remember."

When Christ entered Jerusalem, His path was strewn with leaves of the date palm, a tree that was a sacred emblem to both the Hebrews and the Romans. In fact, it had for centuries been considered one of the most revered symbols of the tree of life in the Garden of Eden. This ceremonial use of the palm established it, in turn, as the foremost living banner of Christianity. It signified triumph over adversity. In the centuries to follow, it was widely used on the tombs of the martyrs interred in the catacombs and in every form of Christian art.

Down through the ages, palm leaves have been distributed each year on Palm Sunday in many Christian churches throughout the world. In some countries both the palm and the olive are used. Palm leaves are also used at the Passover services in the Jewish temples. Most of the palm used on Palm Sunday in the United States is harvested in Florida. Thousands of acres of cattle land in Florida are leased by a single individual for the rights of cutting the buds of the cabbage palm for use on Palm Sunday and in Holy Week services. The cabbage palmetto, as it is commonly referred to, grows in profusion in both salt marsh and fresh water swamps, as well as on hummock land. This palm, which is native to the United States, is the state tree of both Florida and South Carolina. At the top of the tree, deep within the crown of fronds, is the heart of the palm, the terminal bud by which the tree's growth is continued. The bud is protected by a fibrous casing or "bootjack." It is from this point that the great leaves yield the creamy golden spray of new growth which varies from four to six feet. This new growth is the desired form for Palm Sunday.

The bud is sliced from the center of the crown with a palm hook or hatchet, and care is taken not to cut too deeply to avoid injury to the tree. The saw palmetto, *Serenoa repens,* enemy of the cattle rancher, is lower in habit and yields a smaller bud. Approximately three months before Easter, hundreds of workers begin collecting these palm buds from remote swamp lands, which include the 36,000-acre Seminole Indian Reservation. Buds are carefully sorted and, after drying, are wrapped in burlap bags. The cured palms are transferred to huge warehouses for final shipment in refrigerated trucks and railroad cars to churches in various parts of the country.

The rods used to scourge Jesus on His way to Golgotha were cut from a low-growing form of the birch, according to Swedish lore. When the soldiers were fastening Christ to the pillar, they looked about to find switches with which they might scourge Him, for they had been instructed to do this. Seeing the birch nearby, they stripped it of its branches. As a consequence, this tree was struck with a blight, and its descendants are the dwarf birches commonly found carpeting barren land in the colder parts of the world.

Branches from the weeping willow were used for the scourging according to another story. This accounts for the characteristic weeping habit of one of the most beautiful trees seen in parks and gardens everywhere.

On Easter Monday in Czechoslovakia, Pomlázka, the Day of Whipping, a highly popular youth festival is celebrated. Boys braid willow branches into whips, which they festoon with flowers and colored ribbon streamers. The boys then roam about, caroling for eggs and whipping the village girls "so they won't be lazy or have fleas." This is a pre-Christian purification rite and supposedly brings good luck.

Curiously enough, branches of the sallow willow with its showy catkins are often used in English churches on Palm Sunday as a substitute for palm leaves, which can only be obtained by importation from Spain. In the Scandinavian countries, particularly in Denmark, the willow is similarly used.

Along the eastern seaboard of the United States from Ontario and New York to Florida and extending inland to Texas, a showy rosy-pink flowering tree sends forth its pea-like blossoms in spring clustered closely along brown stems. It grows to thirty feet when mature, with leaves that are nearly round. It is called the red-bud, or Judas tree, and closely resembles a species found wild in Palestine, which is one of the trees on which Judas is believed to have hanged himself. In marked contrast, there is the old German myth that Judas, overtaken by remorse, ended his life by hanging himself from the branches of a tall brier rose. The red fruits of this thorny bush are called Judas berries, and presumably the bush was a small tree in form. As with the trees from which the wood of the cross was made, there has been considerable discussion and scholarly argument about the identity of the tree associated with Judas. Was it a fig, the tree which Christ reproved for its failure to produce fruit? Or could it have been a poplar, a brier rose, a black elder, a willow, a terebinth, a carob tree, or a tamarisk? All have been mentioned at various times in past centuries. References to these trees can be found in the writings of Shakespeare, the seventeenth-century herbalists, and collectors of lore of earlier periods.

Charles M. Skinner, noted writer on myths and legends of plants, has recorded a fascinating myth about the willow, which is often called an emblem of sadness. "The willow bears a curse, inasmuch as it is one of the several trees on which Judas hanged himself, being planted by the devil in order to lure people to suicide by the peculiar restful swinging of its branches. It begets snakes, while its ashes drives them away. It is a meeting place and abiding place of witches, for if a witch embarks deliberately on her career of evil, her first step is to a willow, where, sitting on its root, she solemnly forswears God and all holy things; then, writing her name in her own blood on the book that the devil offers, she consigns herself to eternal torment. So, if you shall be tramping a desolate country along between the middle of the night and the break of day, and shall hear a voice luring or laughing from a thicket of willows, beware, for it is Kundry, the witch of 'Parsifal,' who is there. She is that Herodias who asked the head of John the Baptist, and who, as Christ went to His death, laughed at Him. Christ turned one reproving look upon her, then bade her go into the world and wander till his return, forbidding her the solace of tears when she was weary of her fate—a form of the legend of the Wandering Jew."

Every year, toward the end of February, children of all ages watch eagerly for the furry gray catkins of the pussy willows, and on the last Sunday of the month, great sheaves of them are used in some churches in the United States to symbolize the beginning of a new flowering season, the beginning of new life. Young and old alike look forward to taking the canes home after church and rooting them in water to plant them later in their own gardens.

It happens that National Brotherhood Sunday, celebrated in the United States, falls also on this same last Sunday in February, and in some churches, people of different religions worship together on this day. In these instances, the symbolism of the pussy willow is sometimes extended to signify also the brotherly and ancient act of planting together for a new season, striving anew to build together for a better future.

5
Birds in the Easter Story

"As Friday dawned over Jerusalem, other birds besides cocks began to stir and sing, for it was spring, the season of nest-building and of the great migration through Palestine. The aerial flyway above the Holy City was alive with feathered creatures, unaware of what we believe to be the central event of human history taking place below them at Gethsemane, in the palace of Caiaphas, before Pilate's judgment seat, on the rock mound called Golgotha, and in the new stone. In every tree and field and rocky valley near the city were innumerable birds, singing, searching for food, or engaged in their customary springtime activities. But of all of this there is no hint in the account of the darkness that covered the earth during His final three hours on the cross, that nature paused in silent homage as Jesus laid down His life for men. When He died, we are told, nature spoke in the voice of an earthquake and the rending of rocks" —so writes Alice Parmelee in her beautifully conceived and graphically worded *All the Birds of the Bible.*

Into the richly textured tapestry of Easter many emblems and symbols have been woven. Conspicuous throughout all this weaving are the many threads gathered to represent birds. We know that Jesus knew and loved birds, that "His eye is on the sparrow." Besides numerous Scripture references, the folk traditions of many countries have embroidered the factual record with brightly colored legends of the robin, the goldfinch, the crossbill, and other birds. Although the Bible contains no specific reference to the robin, it is believed that the robin of the Old World was a familiar bird in the Holy Land. Cunningham Geikie in *The Life and Words of Christ* has written: "The common sparrow haunts the streets and housetops; swallows and swifts skim the hillsides and the grassy meadows; and, in winter, the robin redbreast abounds." In legend, the robin

Raven

has been closely identified with Christ, and Selma Lagerlöf has perpetuated the tradition in the Swedish legend of "Robin Redbreast."

When God created the world, He not only made heaven and earth, but all the animals and plants as well, giving them all their names. As He painted the birds, He turned to a little creature with gray feathers and said, "Your name will be Robin Redbreast. Although there is no red among your feathers now, you must earn this name, for red is the badge of courage."

Wondering what he might do to earn his feathers, the robin flew into a nearby rose thicket to build his nest. To the other birds of the air, it looked as though he were waiting for a rose petal to fall which would cling to his throat and breast and thus give him the colored vest he so desired. For ever so long he and his fledglings tried in every way possible to earn their promised red breasts. Neither the swelling of its breast in song nor the encounters it had in fighting other birds would spark the color in its breast, and finally all efforts seemed to end in sheer despair.

Then, one world-shaking morning, when the universe seemed in a state of confusion, a courageous robin decided that it was his destiny to earn the coveted red breast so that all who followed him might bear the desired plumage. Determined in his quest, he flew to a hill near Golgotha in the Holy Land. It was shortly after noon, the day Christ was crucified. Happy and hopeful that his mission would be a success, he was soon overwhelmed with sorrow as he witnessed Jesus suffering on a cross made from the trunk of a hawthorn. His heart was filled with sadness when he saw the crown of thorns that the cruel soldiers had placed on Christ's brow. Finally he became so engulfed with pity that, forgetting his timidity and his reluctance to be near people, he flew above the crowd and circled around the cross again and again until, at last, darting down in a sudden burst of courage, he pulled a large thorn from the brow of Christ.

As Robin performed this impulsive act in full view of the soldiers, the blood from the wound made by the thorn oozed out and stained his breast so deeply that when he flew away he was marked with a splash of bright red. There was no mistaking the color or what had made it. When he reached his nest, his family welcomed him, exclaiming as they fluttered about, "The red badge of courage is ours at last!" The red breast which God had foretold must be earned was to be forever the identifying mark of Robin Redbreast.

A companion tale, entitled "Why Robin Redbreast Sings at Easter Time," unfolds another phase of that tragic scene. Despite the fact that Robin had his new plumage, he was dejected and perched by himself in a great cedar of Lebanon, trying to forget the agonizing scene he had just witnessed. Thus, in despair, he remained alone in a far-off corner of Gethsemane until Sunday morning. Finally, he took courage and flew back to the hill of Golgotha, to see what had become of the Saviour. But there was no one about and all vestiges of Friday had disappeared. Yet, the sky was bright and clear and the air was sweet with the perfume of spring flowers carpeting the Palestine hills. But Robin was heavy-hearted. Somehow, his wings instinctively carried him to the very spot where Jesus had been buried. When he reached the place, lo! the stone had been rolled away. And when Robin's small black eyes pierced through the darkness, he saw Christ, in shining robes of whiteness, standing before him.

Immediately the spirit of melancholy left Robin Redbreast and forth from his tiny throat poured a song—and such a song! It was a wondrous melody of love, of joy, of cheer, for Robin sang of life and victory. "The dear Christ is living. I am no longer sorrowful, for from death hath come life. Cheer up, cheer up!" And that is how the robin became the bird to welcome the glad Easter morning with his note of hope, "Cheer up! Cheer up!"

Among the birds depicted in *Holkam Bible Picture Book,* a fourteenth-century manuscript, is the robin. This exceedingly rare volume of early bird drawings is considered one of the most graphic pictorial contributions of the Middle Ages.

Another bird closely connected with Easter is the owl, who signifies solitude. There are at least eight different species of owls that nest in Palestine. This strange "wise" bird who prefers darkness to light has many attributes in the realm of art. His presence conveys the power of Satan, for he brings harm to smaller birds by forcing them into snares set by hunters. Yet, he is thought of as having great wisdom and is often portrayed with hermits like St. Jerome, translator of the Vulgate Bible. A legend concerning the owl weaves its story around the owl as an evil omen. Another tells of a baker's daughter, who, refusing to give bread to Christ, was transformed into an owl. Yet, as George Ferguson points out in *Signs and Symbols of Christian Art,* "In another sense, the owl is the attribute of Christ, who sacrificed Himself to save mankind, 'To give light to them that sit in darkness and in the shadow of death . . .' (Luke 1:79). This explains the presence of the owl in scenes of the Crucifixion."

For centuries, flocks of white pelicans have been found on the shores of the Sea of Galilee. The white pelican is a magnificent bird in flight, with its huge white wingspread and its conspicuous, long, yellowish bill with a crimson tip. However, it is a picture of brooding sorrow as it dolefully sits on a swamp's edge devouring its catch. In Christian art the pelican is not only a symbol of charity, it is used also as an emblem of Christ's sacrifice. The ancient legend associated with the pelican is based on the belief that no bird has greater love for its own offspring, because it pierced its breast to feed its young with its blood. In the early days of the Christian era, Christ's followers saw evidences of His life in all nature, thus the reason for linking the pelican with the passion. In Psalm 102:6 we read, "I am like a pelican of the wilderness." In painting and sculpture, the pelican is sometimes depicted nesting at the top of the cross.

The European goldfinch, often referred to as a "saviour" bird, earned its red face and its habit of eating among thorns and thistles because it too, on witnessing the crucifixion, came to the aid of Christ as He hung on the cross. As a result, this colorful bird has become an accepted symbol of the passion of

Christ. In Tiepolo's "Madonna of the Goldfinch," which hangs in the National Gallery at Washington, the Child is holding a goldfinch in His hand, a symbol of the close association between the incarnation and the passion.

The crossbill, also, was present at the cross of Calvary and while witnessing Christ's agony it struggled desperately to wrench the nails from His hands and feet, only to twist its beak so that its mandibles became crossed in the way it has used them ever since.

In 1603, Schwenckfeld, the noted German mystic, in his *Theriotropheum Silesiae* gave the fable in the Latin verses of Johannes Major, but better known in America is Henry Wadsworth Longfellow's translation from the German of Julius Mosen's "The Legend of the Crossbill," which made the story of this familiar bird very real to people in Victorian days.

> "On the cross the dying Saviour
> Heavenward lifts his eyelids calm,
> Feels, but scarcely feels, a trembling
> In his pierced and bleeding palm.

> "And by all the world forsaken,
> Sees He how with zealous care
> At the ruthless nail of iron
> A little bird is striving there.

> "Stained with blood and never tiring,
> With its beak it doth not cease,
> From the cross 'twould free the Saviour,
> Its Creator's Son release.

> "And the Saviour speaks in mildness:
> 'Blest be thou of all the good!
> Bear, as token of this moment,
> Marks of blood and holy rood!'

> "And that bird is called the crossbill;
> Covered all with blood so clear,
> In the groves of pine it singeth
> Songs, like legends, strange to hear."

The swallow figures prominently in the passion scene. According to an old Scandinavian legend, the swallow flew near the cross, on the day Christ was crucified and, being grief-stricken, yet not knowing what to do, called out *Svale! Svale!* which means "Cheer up! Cheer up!" From then on the swallow has been called the "bird of consolation" and its evening twitterings are soothing sounds. The Scandinavians also believed that, since the swallow was not seen in the winter time, having hibernated in the mud, his emergence in the spring was like a new birth or resurrection. In religious paintings, swallows on the roof serve as an emblem of the Resurrection.

Palestine is unusually rich in bird life. In an Armenian inscription of the fifth century, we learn that in Bible times people enjoyed observing the habits of such birds as swallows, doves, cocks, and eagles. Many swallows remain throughout the year in Palestine, but this is not the case in America. The best known of all the swallow migrations is beautifully told and illustrated by Leo Polito in his *Song of the Swallows*. At the San Juan Mission at Capistrano, California, each spring the entire populace await the arrival of the swallows. The swallows always arrive between two given dates. If they appear on the earlier, the belief is that spring will come early. If they arrive later, so it will be with spring.

Two birds who are ever-present throughout the world and play leading roles in the Scriptures are the dove and the cock. Doves have been abundant everywhere from the beginning of time. Biblical scholars tell us that, during Christ's childhood, doves were sold in the marketplace and that there were dovecotes everywhere in the Holy Land. Jesus, Himself, said that a dove personifying God's Holy Spirit descended and rested upon Him and endowed Him with the spirit of wisdom and understanding, the spirit of counsel and strength, the spirit that knows and reverences God. The dove is symbolic of Christ's own earthly qualities—gentleness, love, purity, humility, swiftness to attain His goal, and willing sacrifice. The emblem of peace, this white bird is a predominant symbol of the Christian church. Its red feet are attributes of the early Christian martyrs. The two creatures that the Devil was believed not to be able to enter were the dove and the lamb.

In the Book of Genesis we read of the dove sent forth from the ark by Noah and the olive branch which he brought back, revealing that the waters had receded and that God and man were at peace. Under Mosaic law, the dove as a symbol of purity explains the presence of the two white doves which Joseph, according to tradition, carried in a basket when Christ was presented in the Temple.

The prime meaning of the dove in Christian art is vested in its symbolism of the Holy Spirit. It is frequently depicted in paintings of the Trinity, the Annunciation, Joseph, the saints, and in other subjects relating to Christ's life. Seven doves represent the seven graces of the Holy Spirit.

The only bird mentioned in the eye-witness reports of the week preceding Easter, is the cock. Jesus said to Peter, "Truly, I say to you, this very night, before the cock crows twice, you will deny me three times." This was reported by all four Gospel writers, Mark, Matthew, Luke, and John. And as Friday dawned over Jerusalem, and the birds began to stir (for it was spring, and daylight came early), the cock crowed and again we learn from all four chroniclers that "immediately the cock crowed a second time. And Peter remembered how Jesus had said to him Before the cock crows twice, you will deny Me three times. And he broke down and wept."

It was Job who queried, "Who hath given understanding to the cock?" In classical mythology the cock was dedicated to Apollo, the sun god, because it

Cock calling hens

gave notice of the rising of the sun; to Mercury because it summoned men to business by its crowing; and to Aesculapius, the son of Apollo, because "early to bed and early to rise, makes a man healthy." According to a Mohammedan legend, the Prophet found in the first heaven a cock of such enormous size that its crest touched the second heaven. The crowing of this celestial bird aroused every living creature from sleep except man. The Moslem doctors say that Allah lends a willing ear to him who reads the Koran, to him who prays for pardon, and to the cock whose chant is "divine melody." When this cock ceases to crow, the Day of Judgment will be at hand.

Unearthed in Palestine was Jaazaniah's seal on which was engraved a fighting cock, the date on the seal, 587 B.C. Jaazaniah was one of Zedekiah's captains of the armies who came to Mizpah after the King's defeat by Nebuchadnezzar. Cock-fighting has been a popular diversion down through the ages. The noted English folklorist Christina Hole has written: "In England cock-fighting was a traditional sport of the season both for adults and children. Fitz-Stephen, writing in the twelfth century, tells us that yearly at Shrovetide the boys of every school bring fighting-cocks to their masters, and all the forenoon is spent at school, to see these cocks fight together. As late as the beginning of the last century, a fee called the cock-penny was paid by scholars to the schoolmaster, so that he could buy birds for this purpose. Cock-fighting is, of course, illegal now as are also some other brutal Shrovetide pastimes, like thrashing the hen and throwing at tethered cocks."

Cock-fighting still exists in Latin countries, and we find in ceramics, in tin, and in other materials many an Easter figurine fashioned in the shape of a rooster. In Italy and Portugal Easter cakes are often molded in the form of this bird. Besides the ceramic roosters of Portugal and the tin ones made in Mexico, the Swedes fashion them out of wood and paint them handsomely.

The hen's importance is prevalent universally for its production of eggs for Easter eggs. Jesus spoke of the hen and its chickens in this reference, Luke 13:34: "O Jerusalem, Jerusalem, which killest the prophets, and stonest them that are sent unto thee; how often would I have gathered thy children together, as a hen doth gather her brood under her wings, and ye would not!"

Only in America do we find toy replicas of chickens being used extensively for Easter decoration—it would sometimes seem that for every candy Easter egg made there is a small yellow or white cuddly, cotton chick. Florence Hoatson in her little verse entitled "Yellow," tells us where the color originated.

"Of all the colours God has made
I love the pretty yellow shade—
The colour of canaries' wings,
Of baby chicks, and fluffy things;
I think He must have spilt the sun
Upon the darlings, every one!"

The bird that appears as often in the Bible as the dove is the eagle. The eagle symbolized God's care of His people. The eagle legend is also related closely to that of the phoenix, for, like the phoenix, the eagle is possessed of remarkable qualities. It was thought that the eagle restored its life by flying so close to the sun that its feathers were scorched and burned. While still burning, the eagle would plunge downward into water and miraculously the plumage would be renewed or restored. Thus, the eagle, as well as the phoenix, symbolized the rebirth of mankind, through the Crucifixion and the Resurrection of Christ. The golden eagle and the spread eagle commonly used for symbols in decoration are commemorative of the Crusades.

Pelican

The fabled incorruptibility of the peacock's flesh caused this bird to be adopted, for a while, to supplant the phoenix, as an emblem of the Resurrection. From the curious notion that peacock flesh does not decay came the use of the peacock as an emblem of immortality. Not only did the peacock appear on monuments and in windows, but, we learn from the writings of Anastasius, an early Pope, that the variegated feathers of the bird, or imitations of them in embroidery, were often used in early times as decorations in churches. The wings of angels, also, were often represented as formed of the feathers of the peacock.

Although peacocks are non-migratory, they are known throughout the world today. Phoenician traders brought them from India to Egypt before Solomon's time, but the three Bible references to these birds are believed to be the oldest written records of them outside India. When a Roman empress died, a peacock was released from her funeral pyre, as a sign that she had become a goddess and was immortal. In like manner, an eagle was released upon the death ceremony of an emperor. Wherever a peacock sign is found on an inn in England, it hangs there as a remembrance of the Crusades. The bird was adopted by many knights as a crest typical of the Resurrection. "By the Peacock" was a favorite oath of the day. Today, when the Pope is carried in his processional chair, two chamberlains on either side of him bear flabelli—great fans of ostrich plumes tipped with peacock feathers and mounted on long poles.

The phoenix, the oldest known bird of mythological and literary renown, has been universally adopted as the symbol of immortality and as such appears on some church calendars on Easter Day. There is hardly a race that did not have its own legend and beliefs about the phoenix. Although many references call the phoenix "a fabulous Arabian bird," it probably owed its imaginary existence to the Egyptians. Immortality was bestowed on this bird because, unlike the other birds in the Garden of Eden, it did not eat the forbidden fruit.

Tacitus and Pliny, although they made no claim of having seen the phoenix themselves, said that a bird had been seen. In the first century St. Clement narrated the phoenix legend in his first Epistle to the Corinthians and this mythological bird was adopted as a Christian symbol of the Resurrection.

"The myth of the phoenix" (remarks George Stephens in *Archaeologia*) "is

Phoenix

one of the most ancient in the world. Originally a temple type of the immortality of the soul, its birthplace appears to have been the sunny clime of the fanciful and gorgeous East. Even in the days of Job and David, it was already a popular tradition in Palestine and Arabia. Afterwards it passed over to Egypt, Greece and Rome; but, as it went, lost feather after feather, until the spiritual, delicate and beautiful parable sank into the tangible folk-lore of a nine day wonder. The fathers of the Christian Church were the first to restore it to its original form and hidden meaning."

It was Herodotus who described the phoenix (which he admitted he had never seen) as a bird with plumage partly red and partly golden whose general make and size were comparable to that of an eagle. The bird came all the way from Arabia and brought the parent bird all plastered over with myrrh to the Temple of the Sun in Egypt where he buried the body.

This fabulous winged creature was believed to live as long as five hundred years. When it observes that it is growing old, it collects branches from spice trees and builds itself a funeral pyre. On this, twining its body toward the rays of the sun and flapping its wings, it sets fire to itself of its own accord until it burns itself up. On the ninth day afterward, it rises from its own ashes, having emerged from an egg deposited in the ashes before death.

The ancient tradition of the phoenix has given the name to whatever is singular and uncommon in its kind. Thus, a truly accomplished person may be called a phoenix. Queen Elizabeth I used a phoenix on her medals and she herself has been compared frequently in prose and poetry to this extraordinary bird.

The phoenix represents faith and constancy in symbolism and was commonly used in painting and sculpture in the Middle Ages, but it apparently had little appeal or symbolism to the artists of the Renaissance. It is still used on certain church vestments in a variety of conventionalized forms—the silhouette of a bird rising out of flames.

Another winged creature, although not a bird, has its own important role in the Easter story. The butterfly is often used as an Easter symbol, because its entire life cycle parallels that of Christ. First, the caterpillar stage stands for life; second, the cocoon or chrysalis signifies death; and the third stage, that of the butterfly emerging from the cocoon, portrays the Resurrection. The butterfly is often seen in religious art, but this resplendent moth usually appears later in the season in many countries than Easter. Consequently, we lose sight of this image.

6
Animals in the Easter Story

Strangely enough, there is a dearth of folklore and legend concerning animals and especially the part which they play in the story of Easter. Yet, several beasts have important roles in this greatest of feasts. The symbolism of the lamb was so intimate a part of the everyday life of the time in which Christ lived that probably there was little need for fanciful tales to point up its importance in the episodes of the Saviour's passion.

The donkey was a commonplace beast of burden. His docility, his slow plodding manner, and his woebegone expression were the butt of jokes and stories then, as now, so that a few of such tales have become a part of the realm of folklore.

As for the rabbit, there is little to say about him relating to the time of Christ. There were no rabbits in the Holy Land, but the hare, which closely resembles the rabbit, was abundant in Palestine more than nineteen hundred years ago.

The myths and legends and the symbolism to which these animals are related have been gathered over the centuries since the time of Christ's life on earth. New ways of telling them, or the mere gathering together of these old tales, represent an attempt to assemble as many facets as possible of the Easter story.

Of all the symbols of Easter, the lamb is the most familiar and, doubtless, it ranks next in importance to the cross itself. Jesus is portrayed frequently as a shepherd carrying a lamb on his shoulders. Since sheepherding was one of the chief occupations of the ancient Hebrews, this image of the Master conveyed a feeling of warmth and love which made the Twenty-third Psalm vibrant with meaning. Folklorists remind us continually that the lamb was known as the only animal that the Devil could not enter. For this reason and many others, the lamb is an important motif in the tapestry of Easter.

In John 1:29 we read, "The next day John seeth Jesus coming unto him, and saith, Behold the Lamb of God which taketh away the sin of the world." Christ as the kindly shepherd rescuing the lamb personifies the Saviour and the sinner —a picture so simple in its beauty of concept that the early Christians who saw the Master in everything came to love it, for it made Christ's life very real to them. We find the lamb frequently appearing in Christian art with the Holy Family, John the Baptist, and others.

The paschal lamb of the Jewish Passover became a symbol of Christ, following the first Easter. Since the lamb was always used as the sacrificial animal, the parallel in symbolism was easy to establish. Thus Jesus, as the Lamb of God, was made the supreme sacrifice on the cross.

The Vesper Hymn of Easter proclaims:

> "The Lamb's high banquet we await
> In snow-white robes of royal state;
> And now, the Red Seas channel past,
> To Christ our Prince we sing at last.
> That Paschal Eve God's arm was bared,
> The devastating Angel spared;
> By strength of hand our hosts went free
> From Pharaoh's ruthless tyranny.
> O Thou, from whom hell's monarch flies,
> O great, O very Sacrifice,
> Thy captive people are set free,
> And endless life restored in thee."

One of the most familiar symbols of Easter is the lamb carrying a banner with a red cross superimposed on it. In stonework, stained glass, and embroidery, it is one of the commonest themes of religious art, and references to the lamb in Christian scripture and worship are so frequent that, next to the cross itself, the lamb is probably the most important symbol of Christianity. In England it is a cherished belief of ancient origin that the image of the lamb and the banner appeared in the center of the sun's disk on Easter morning. Since it was visible only in the first few moments after the sun had risen, country folk used to go to bed early on Easter Saturday night so that they might rise early enough to go to some nearby promontory to see it.

In Finland, Easter lambs made of wax, supposed to have magical protective powers, are distributed by the pastor to his parishioners. Lambs of gold or silver are used in Finland as charms and are worn on chains. Cakes are made in the shape of lambs in Italy, Czechoslovakia, and in the United States to be used at Easter. Candies of spun sugar in the shape of lambs are the Easter joy of the children in Sicily and other European countries.

Next to the lamb, the donkey has a well-established place in Christian tradition. The humblest of all beasts was chosen to carry Christ. It was on the back of an ass that Mary rode to Bethlehem where she was delivered of the Messiah. The same beast was the one upon which she and the Christ Child, with Joseph, made their escape from Herod into Egypt. Years later, it was an ass that Christ rode when He made His triumphal entry into Jerusalem. Riding an ass meant that He came as a peaceful conqueror and not as a warrior. And, legend has it that during His crucifixion, the ass watched the scene and was bowed down with grief. Ever since, there is to be found a dark patch of hair that goes the length of the donkey's back and another that crosses his shoulders, thus marking the cross simulating Christ's passion.

Two modern stories relate the donkey legend with great feeling. In *Donkey's Glory*, by Nan Goodall, we learn of a prophecy: "The little gray donkey shall be a King's play fellow, and her daughter shall see wonderful things; but the snow-white donkey shall carry the King in His triumph, and everybody shall laugh and sing." *Trottemenu* (the traditional French medieval name of the ass) was the name of the ass that was a playfellow for the Child Jesus. And Trottemenu's grandson Laban (Hebrew for white) was the donkey destined to carry Jesus as king into Jerusalem.

The second fable is *The Donkey Who Always Complained*, by Francis Beauchesne Thornton, a talented raconteur. This swift-moving story, a "parable for moderns," is a tale at once simple and poetic, of the lowly beast that carried Christ into Jerusalem on the first Palm Sunday. Balo, the donkey of this tale, and her forebears, have been present at other great moments in the life of the Family of Nazareth, and what these animals see and hear is related in this touching story.

Selma Lagerlöf tells us that at the beginning of the world, when all things were created, the donkey got his long ears because he could not remember the name that had been given to him. No sooner had he taken a few steps over the meadows of Eden than he forgot, and three times he had to return to inquire what his name was. At last God grew somewhat impatient and taking him by his two ears, said, "Thy name is ass, ass, ass!" And, while He thus spoke, He pulled both of the ass's ears that he might hear better and remember what was said to him.

Gilbert Keith Chesterton, who charmed the reading public of the English-speaking world with his verse during the first third of the twentieth century, has given us this unforgettable picture of "The Donkey":

> "When fishes flew and forest walked
>   And figs grew upon thorn,
> Some moment when the moon was blood
>   Then surely I was born.
>
> "With monstrous head and sickening cry
>   And ears like errant wings,
> The devil's walking parody
>   On all four-footed things.

"The tattered outlaw of the earth,
Of ancient crooked will;
Starve, scourge, deride me: I am dumb
I keep my secret still.

"Fools! For I also had my hour;
One far fierce hour and sweet:
There was a shout about my ears,
And palms before my feet."

A lion was the emblem of the tribe of Judah, and Christ is called "the lion of the tribe of Judah." According to tradition, the lion's whelp is born dead and remains so for three days, at which time the sire breathes on it and it receives life. From this myth the lion came to be associated with the Resurrection. The lion signifies strength, majesty, and courage, in contrast to the leopard, which personifies sin. Another folk belief is that the lion is the only member of the cat tribe born with its eyes open, and it is said that it sleeps with its eyes open. This, of course, is mere fiction, but this long-held notion gave the lion stature as the spirit of watchfulness. On the other hand, his reputation for ferociousness suggested his association with the Devil. A lion found at the feet of crusaders or martyrs in effigy signifies that they died for the Master's cause. Mark, the Evangelist, is symbolized by a lion because he begins his Gospel with the scenes of John the Baptist and Christ in the wilderness. (Venice, the city of which St. Mark is patron, uses the lion as its emblem.)

The pig offers its meat as a traditional Easter dish. This animal has always been a symbol of good luck and prosperity among the Indo-Europeans. Many traces of this ancient symbolism are still alive in our time. In some German popular expressions, the word "pig" is synonymous with "good luck" (*Schwein haben*). Piggy banks carry out the ancient symbolism of good luck and prosperity.

The whale is referred to as an Easter symbol, for it was believed that the story of Jonah was a prophecy foretelling the course of events in the life of Christ. In the Old Testament we read that for three days Jonah lay in the belly of a great fish (the whale) and then was cast up on dry land, unharmed. Similarly, Jesus lay dead for three days in the tomb and then rose and came forth again into the light of the world. An ancient belief associates the whale with the Devil, and the whale, when depicted with his mouth open, represented the gates of hell.

The Germans have a tradition that when Christ was crucified all the fishes dived under the waters in terror, except the pike, which out of curiosity lifted up its head and beheld the whole scene. Hence, we have the fancy that in a pike's head all the parts of the crucifixion are represented; a cross, three nails, and a sword being distinctly recognizable.

The sand dollar or Holy Ghost shell, one of the animals of the sea, commonly found on sandy beaches when the tide goes out, has distinctive marks in which can be seen symbols of the birth, the crucifixion, and the Resurrection of Christ. On the top side of the shell, an outline of the Easter lily is clearly seen, and in the center of the lily appears a five-pointed star representing the star of Bethlehem. The five narrow openings are representative of the four nail holes and the spear wound made in the body of Christ during the crucifixion. Reversing the shell, it is easy to recognize the outline of the Christmas poinsettia and the bell. When broken, we find inside the shell five little birds called the doves of peace. Some legends claim that they are the angels that sang to the shepherds on the first Christmas morning.

In America the lovable Easter bunny has become the children's symbol of this festive season, since it is commonly believed that he brings the colorful Easter eggs and other gifts. The term "bunny" is commonly used to mean "rabbit." He is similar in many ways to the hare of European history, lore, and myth. A rabbit differs from a hare in the formation of its skull, the length of its ears, and the length of its hind legs. Rabbits seek cover in burrows, whereas the hare takes off as in flight. Further comparison indicates that the rabbit is born underground and is blind at birth. The hare, on the other hand, is usually born in a form or nest above ground, with its eyes open. Rabbits may produce a half-dozen litters of young each year, the average litter ranging from five to seven. No better example of a symbol of fertility can be found in the animal kingdom than the rabbit.

This four-footed creature was once a bird, but *Eostre,* the dawn goddess, known in Sanskrit as Usra, made the transformation. The association of the hare with the moon, which governs the setting of the date for Easter, is obvious. "Catching the hare" was a custom at the festival of the Easter goddess, and the hare was the emblem of Aphrodite, the goddess of love, in Greece. He may also be connected with the corn-spirit, because in many parts of Europe the last sheaf of corn to be cut is called the "hare," and the cutting is sometimes called "cutting the tail of the hare."

The hare, being the most prolific of animals, is a prime symbol of fertility. The bunny is really a hare, and the hare is a symbol of the moon, according to legends in Egypt. Everyone knows that the date of Easter is determined by the moon. In the year A.D. 325, Constantine had the uncertain date of this settled for all time by taking the matter before the Council of Nicea. The astronomers of Alexandria, Egypt, experts in calculating dates that were governed by the course of the heavenly bodies, were authorized by the Council to help the archbishop of Alexandria determine for the whole church the date of Easter. It was agreed that Easter should fall upon the first Sunday after the first full moon after the twenty-first day of March.

In Texas, during the observance of the Easter Fire, the children are told that it is the Easter rabbit burning wild flowers to make dyes for the Easter eggs. The canejo, or "painted" rabbit, is the one which the children of Panama believe brings the Easter eggs.

In England, the ritual of hunting the hare once took place in the spring season. In Yugoslavia, the hare makes a nest in the stable, and there the young folk go on Easter morning to find the eggs concealed in the hay. In England, they hunt in the garden, in the long grasses, and among the spring flowers. No matter where the hare is sought, he reappears in his ancient guise, as the living emblem of fertility, renewal, and the return of spring.

In America, cakes, cookies, and candies are made into the shape of Easter bunnies, and every store has all sorts of bunny toys: plush bunnies, cotton bunnies, plastic bunnies, and, sad to state, real live bunnies for sale. The Society for Prevention of Cruelty to Animals pleads with all to stop the sale of the live bunny, for all too often the small creature is taken from its mother too early, thus placing a tax not only upon the little rabbit but also upon its recipient.

It is said that when Easter is celebrated in the northern parts of the United States, it is apt to appear wrapped in white bunny fur! Certainly the white fur of the Easter bunny is a welcome sight, even if the spring snow is not! In *The Easter Book,* by Francis Weiser he states, "The Easter bunny has never had a religious symbolism bestowed on its festive usage, though its white meat is sometimes said to suggest purity and innocence."

In Germany, as important to children as St. Nicholas is to Christmas is the role the Easter rabbit plays at Easter time—in fact, some argue that the Easter bunny is the more important. The earliest recorded mention of the Easter rabbit and his eggs is a short admonition in a German book of the late sixteenth century. "Do not worry if the bunny escapes you; should we miss his eggs then we shall cook the nest." In a German book dated 1682, the story that the Easter bunny lays eggs and hides them in the garden is called "an old fable." Also, from Germany comes the note that the Easter bunny was believed to lay red eggs on Maundy Thursday and eggs of other colors on Easter eve.

Several authors of children's books have contributed to the universal place of love that the rabbit holds in the affections of the peoples of the world. The noted English writer, Beatrix Potter, with her inimitable *Tale of Peter Rabbit,* awakened people to the bunnies and inspired many writers. In America this rabbit lore has been greatly increased by Joel Chandler Harris with his *Bre'r Rabbit Tales,* Thornton W. Burgess by his *Adventures of Peter Cottontail,* and Robert Lawson, whose devotion to rabbits shines forth from his *Rabbit Hill,* in which the rabbits wistfully hope that the new occupants of the house will welcome spring as "growing-folks."

In a recent article in *Friar,* a religious magazine, Ade Bethune, noted authority on religious art, posed the question, " 'Has the Easter bunny become a menace to the Paschal season?' Sticklers for realism are apt to disapprove of him. 'As if it weren't bad enough,' they figure, 'to disgrace the holy season with a silly rabbit, how in heaven's name do you reconcile the creature with the Easter egg?'

"Some parents will let their children have the eggs, but put their foot down against the bunny. And, yet, it's hard to avoid him. Come spring, and lo, from every store and poster over the land he stares at you. Every child in vernal finery who is not seen carrying a potted hyacinth to grandmother is at least clutching a lavender stuffed toy twice his own size and ornamented with large overhanging ears.

" 'Christmas already has been all but ruined by the Santa Claus cult, and now Easter in turn is being subverted,' so our friends of realism are apt to complain. But, as far as I am concerned, they are missing the proverbial boat.

"The rabbit's burrow, like the tomb wherein Christ lay, is a dark hole in the earth. From this 'tomb' he too arises, and with bounding agility skims over hill and dale, a figure of our bodies as they will rise on the Last Day in the likeness of our Risen Lord.

"If you be risen with Christ, seek the things that are above, and as you do so, incidentally, see in the rabbit, not so many pounds of meat and fur, but also the springing joy of the spirit alert to God's ways."

H. Armstrong Roberts

7
Foods of the Easter Season

Food plays an important role in the observance of Lent, which culminates on Easter Day, the "Feast of Feasts." To folk whose background and inheritance are closely allied with the Old World, the traditional foods of the Lenten season have a special kind of appeal. They help recall old customs that are closely associated with the preparation and serving of these old-time dishes. They are, in part, symbols of the season and in many cases are linked with religious customs and practices which bring to mind some facet of the Lenten observance.

Some of the recipes presented in this chapter are written in the manner of the period in which they were popular, but they are easily adaptable to present-day use. Sugar designated in recipes is granulated unless otherwise specified.

Egg Saturday, Collop Monday, and Pancake Tuesday have colorful backgrounds steeped in tradition. *Fastnachts,* pretzels, dandelion greens, fig pudding, simnel cake, furmety, *mayvutsa, kulich, posna zupa,* and a whole pantryful of other foods have a nostalgic ring for those who have cooked and eaten them, or at least sampled them on one occasion or another. These foods are all good eating, and worth a try come Lent.

Shrovetide, in both church and folk tradition, is the English name for the last four days before the beginning of Lent: Egg Saturday, Quinquagesima Sunday, Collop Monday, and Shrove Tuesday. In bygone days on Egg Saturday, the first day of Shrovetide, the children went lent-crocking, demanding gifts of eggs or meat, and hurling broken crockery at the doors of those who refused them.

On Collop Monday, eggs and collops appeared on the table for the last time before Lent. The term "collop" referred to pieces of meat, such as ham, bacon,

or any other meat that was cured by being salted or hung to dry, in contrast to the term "steaks" for slices of fresh meat. It was a day when pot-luck meant infinite variety, a little of this and a little of that. But one fact was certain, there would be no more meat served until Lent was over.

Egg Collops

4 hard-cooked eggs
Pepper and salt to taste
2 tbsp. grated cheese
½ cup thick white sauce (made with cream)

2 beaten eggs
2 tbsp. flour
3 tbsp. fine bread crumbs

Shell and chop the hard-cooked eggs. Add pepper and salt, grated cheese, and white sauce. Bind with a little beaten egg to a stiff paste. With floured hands, form the mixture into cock shapes. Roll in beaten egg and then in bread crumbs. Fry to a golden brown in hot fat. Garnish with buttered peas and buttered parslied carrots.

Shrove Tuesday, or Pancake Day, is the Tuesday before Ash Wednesday. The bell that once called the churchgoers to confession—that is, to be "shriven" —or have one's sins forgiven, became known as the Pancake Bell, and Shrove Tuesday was also called Pancake Day. In England, this same day is sometimes called "Goodish" or "Goodies" Day because of the many good things to eat. In France, the day is referred to as Bannock Tuesday, and in parts of the United States (where it is the last day of Mardi Gras) it ends with the Burying of the Sardine as described in Chapter 9.

There are two celebrated pancake ceremonies in England. At Westminster School a pancake is annually scrambled for in the ceremony known as the Pancake Greeze. At eleven o'clock on Shrove Tuesday morning, the cook, preceded by the verger with the silver-topped mace, enters the Great Schoolroom, carrying a frying pan from which he tosses a pancake over the high bar separating the old Upper and Lower Schools. The assembled boys scramble for it as it falls to the ground, and he who secures it, or the largest part of it, receives a guinea from the Dean. The cook is also rewarded for his essential part in the affair. At one time, all the boys in the school took part in the scramble, but now each form chooses one of its members to represent it.

Throughout England, children sing this song on Pancake Day:

> "Dibbity, dibbity, dibbity, doe,
> Give me a pancake and I'll go,
> Dibbity, dibbity, dibbity, ditter,
> Please to give me a bit of a fritter."

The other Pancake Day ceremony concerns a race. In England, in bygone days, it was the custom for the housewives to drop whatever they were doing and hurry to the church at the tolling of the bell on each Shrove Tuesday. In 1445, a wife in Olney, England, started baking her pancakes rather late on

Shrove Tuesday. The pancakes she was making were flat cakes made in a frying pan, and would be eaten to sustain her, for she would have a long wait to be shriven on that day. The pancakes were not quite finished when the church bell rang, but she hurried off to her "shriving," carrying her griddle and pancakes with her. Thus an annual sporting event was born.

In Liberal, Kansas, this five-hundred-year-old event of pancake racing, which consisted of racing over a 415-yard course from the "town pump" to the church, became a challenge. In 1950, urged on by the local Junior Chamber of Commerce, the housewives of Liberal challenged the housewives of Olney, Bucks, England, to a pancake race. The British housewives, through the Reverend R. C. Collins, Vicar of Olney, accepted the challenge. For the running of what has now become the international Pancake Day Race, over courses of identical distance, times of the winners in both Olney and Liberal are compared by trans-Atlantic telephone.

Pancake Day in Liberal, Kansas, has reached staggering proportions, and several days of festivities are now scheduled. This is the pancake rhyme from Liberal:

> "Shrove Tuesday's the day (it happens each year)
> Pancakes are flipping—far and near
> Promoting world friendship
> Good cheer and good will . . .
> Come help us celebrate
> Eat to your fill . . .
> And when the day's over
> You'll remember it long,
> You, filled with pancakes,
> Your heart with a song."

Shrovetide Pancakes

2 cups allpurpose flour	2 eggs (yolk and white beaten together)
Pinch of salt	Milk to make batter thin

Mix together flour, salt, well-beaten eggs, and just enough milk to make the batter thin. Have greased griddle very hot. Put 4 tbsp. of batter into a teacup and pour onto the griddle. Bake until golden brown on one side, then turn over and bake on the other.

Car-Cake

A small cake made with eggs and cooked on a griddle, and eaten on Shrove Tuesday in parts of Scotland and northern England. Sometimes served to children as a highly flavored pancake. A blood car-cake is a cake mixed with hog's blood and eaten on Easter Sunday.

A *fastnacht* is served on Shrove Tuesday. A genuine *fastnacht kuche* is made without yeast and the omission of yeast was considered very important by our

 ancestors. Shrove Tuesday is a significant day in the church calendar of the Old World and in parts of America where ancient customs are still cherished. Traditionally the *fastnacht kuche* is baked only once a year—on Shrove Tuesday or on the Monday before. The important fact is that it be eaten on Shrove Tuesday, although a sufficient quantity is generally baked to last the rest of the week, provided that the family appetite is not too large. Anything baked with raised dough is not a *fastnacht kuche*, regardless of when it is baked or how it is shaped. The following recipe from *Eastertide in Pennsylvania* by Alfred L. Shoemaker, published by the Pennsylvania Folklife Society, Kutztown, Pennsylvania, has been used by the Pennsylvania Dutch for generations.

Genuine Fastnacht Kuche

¾ cup thick sour cream ¼ cup sugar
¾ cup thick sour milk 1 egg
1½ tsp. baking soda

Mix ingredients. Stiffen with enough flour to roll. Roll about ¼ inch thick and cut into desired shape and size—2-inch squares are preferable. Fry in deep fat. The amount of sugar may be increased, but this is not necessary if eaten in the approved manner.

To eat, split the *fastnacht kuche* in half and fill the inside with *gwidde hunnich* (quince jam). To use anything as ordinary and common as molasses on a genuine *fastnacht kuche* is an abomination. In the absence of *gwidde hunnich,* crabapple jelly may be substituted.

The pretzel was originally made as a Lenten food in Austria, Germany, and Poland, and always made its appearance on Ash Wednesday. Pretzel is the German contraction for the Latin word meaning "littlearms." This baked dough was made to take the place of bread, for it must be remembered that milk, eggs, and fats were forbidden during Lent. Pretzels, which are enjoyed at any time of year, were first made in the fifth century A.D. The dough, made of flour, salt, and water, is twisted in such a manner as to represent two arms crossed in the act of prayer. When the pretzels were eaten, they were remindful of the reverence associated with the season of Lent, and for many years this was the only time they were eaten. They were given to the paupers of the town in place of bread on certain days of Lent.

Postna Zupa—Lenten Soup—Poland

4 carrots 2 sprigs parsley
4 stalks celery 2 tbsp. butter
1 onion 2 qts. cold water
Salt and pepper

Wash vegetables, cut into small pieces, and sauté in butter, under cover, until they are browned. Add water and seasonings and simmer for half-hour. Strain before serving.

Irish Lenten Cake (Eggless)

½ cup (¼ lb.) butter
3 tbsp. molasses
1 cup milk
4 cups sifted flour
¾ cup sugar
3 tsp. allspice
2 tsp. baking powder
1 tsp. baking soda
½ tsp. salt
½ cup raisins

Melt butter, add molasses and milk, and cool. Sift flour, sugar, spice, baking powder, baking soda, and salt. Stir butter mixture into dry ingredients. Add raisins and mix well. Pour into buttered tin and bake 1½ hours in a 350° oven.

Several generations of children have enjoyed Margery Clark's *Poppy Seed Cakes* (still available in anthologies of favorite stories). If, with the coming of spring you have a yen for Auntie Katuska's poppy seed cakes, here is the Old World recipe.

Poppy Seed Muffins (Cakes)

2 cups flour
3 tsp. baking powder
1 tbsp. sugar
½ tsp. salt
2 eggs (unbeaten)
4 tbsp. melted shortening
1 cup milk
2 tsp. poppy seeds

Sift dry ingredients together; add unbeaten eggs, melted shortening which has been cooled, and milk to make a stiff batter. Add poppy seeds; mix well. Half fill greased muffin tins and bake in hot oven (400°) for 18 to 20 minutes. Makes 12 muffins.

America's contribution to Lenten (fatless) breads:

Orange Bread

1 large orange, grated
Juice of 1 orange
1 cup sugar
3 cups flour
1 tsp. salt
4 level tsp. baking powder
3 tbsp. sugar
1 egg
1 cup milk

Cook together for a little while the grated orange, the orange juice, and the cup of sugar. Then add to other ingredients. Mix together. Bake 45 minutes in 350° oven.

The fourth Sunday in Lent is called "Mothering Sunday" in European countries. On mid-Lent Sunday in England, the parishioners in outlying hamlets, who normally worshiped in chapels-of-ease (as the small churches of the great houses were called), went to the mother church of the parish, bringing their offerings. How early the idea of honoring one's own mother on that particular day began is not certain.

On Mothering Sunday, above all, it was customary that every child should dine with its mother. This pleasant custom dates from the sixteenth century. In those days young girls who had hired out as servants for the first time at

the New Year hiring fairs were given a holiday in mid-Lent so that they could visit their families. To prove their cooking skill, they brought home a gift of a "mothering" or "simnel" cake. And because the Lenten fast in those times was rigorous, they used a rich mixture so that the cake would keep until Easter.

As well as evidence of her newly acquired cooking skill, the girl sometimes brought home for family approval her newly acquired sweetheart. And, if she happened to be a dairy maid or laundry maid, the sweetheart bought or had made for her the mothering cake. There is an old verse which goes:

> "And I'll to thee a simnel bring
> 'Gainst thou goest a-mothering;
> So that when she blesses thee
> Half the blessing thou'st give me."

In "Richard Symonds Diary" (1644) may be found the quotation: "Every Mid-Lent Sunday is a great day, when all the children and grandchildren meet at the head and chief of the family and have a feast."

John Brandt writes that "it was customary in the eighteenth and early nineteenth centuries, for servants or others working away from home to be given a holiday then, so that they might visit their mothers and present them with a cake of their own or their mistress's making, and little nosegays of violets and other wild flowers gathered in the hedgerows as they walked along the country lanes. Whole families attended church together and there was a dinner of roast lamb or veal, at which mother was treated as queen of the feast she had prepared herself, and everything was done to make her happy." This custom never reached the shores of the Americas, for the idea of Mother's Day, the second Sunday of May, was conceived much later. Mother is feted—the token is only a carnation—there are always gifts.

The cakes made for mothers were called simnels. The name "simnel" is derived from simila, a fine wheaten flour. There are two legends connected with this name. One relates that the father of Lambert Simnel (one of the two false pretenders to the throne in Henry VII's reign), a baker, concocted a certain cake and named it for his notorious son. The other account states that a man named Simon, and Nell, his wife, quarreled as to whether the mixture (cake) should be baked or boiled. They compromised by doing both, and since then the cake has been known by a combination of their two names.

Simnel Cake

A description of a simnel cake: "The crust was made of flour, water and saffron, to envelop a filling of mixed plums, lemon peel and many good things. The edges were pinked, the top duly criss-crossed, the whole boiled in a cloth, then glazed with egg and finally baked." The cakes were sold at a guinea apiece and were so large and so hard that it is small wonder that one mother new to the region used hers for a footstool!

Simnel Cake (Modern Version)

Cream together 1 cup (½ lb.) butter with 1 cup sugar. Sift 2 cups flour with 1 tsp. grated nutmeg, 1 tsp. ground cinnamon, 1 tsp. ground ginger, ½ tsp. salt, and 2 tsp. baking powder. With 2½ cups raisins and 2 cups currants mix ¾ cup cherries and ¾ cup chopped candied peel. Beat 4 eggs, add 2 tbsp. milk and 1 tsp. vanilla. Work beaten eggs into creamed mixture. Gradually add half the flour, then add all the fruit, finally mix in remainder of flour (mixture should be fairly stiff). Line a 9-inch tin with several thicknesses of wax paper. Put half the mixture into the tin, smoothing the top evenly. Over this place a half-inch round of almond paste. Add remainder of mixture, smoothe top, and bake in a slow oven (325°) for 4 hours.

When cake is cool, cut out another round of almond paste exactly the size of cake. Cut a three-inch round from the center and place the ring of paste on top of the cake. Form a number of small balls or eggs (11 is the traditional number) with the remainder of the paste and lay these at intervals on the ring of almond paste. Brush with beaten egg and place in a hot oven (500°) for 2½ minutes, or until paste is slightly brown. When cold, fill the center of the cake with glacé frosting. When this is set, use a pastry tube to decorate the cake with an appropriate greeting.

Glacé Frosting for Simnel Cake

    1 cup sieved confectioner's sugar   2 tbsp. water
              1 tbsp. strained lemon juice

Combine ingredients in top of double boiler and stir over hot water until sugar is melted. The frosting should be only warm. While still warm, pour over cake.

Almond Paste (Marzipan)

    3½ cups sifted confectioner's sugar   4 eggs (beaten)
    5 cups ground almonds   Juice of 1 lemon
    1 cup sugar   1 tsp. vanilla
              1 tsp. each, rum and orange-flower water

Crush confectioner's sugar with rolling pin and sieve well. Mix dry ingredients. Beat the eggs and add gradually with the flavorings. Mix to a paste, first with a wooden spoon and then with the hand. A word of caution: While it is essential to work the marzipan into a smooth paste, it must not be overhandled or it will become crumbly and bitter and difficult to roll and mold. Having kneaded the paste, wrap it in wax paper, put it in a covered tin, and leave it until the following day when it will be easier to handle.

Today in England, mid-Lent wafers are served in the place of simnels. At the Winchester Museum, 300-year-old wafering irons are taken out of safe-keeping so that the ecclesiastical symbols of the letters I H S (Jesus Hominum Salvator) may be pressed on one side. The wafers are cooked by pouring batter onto the bottom plate of the wafering irons pre-heated in a wood fire.

Another special dish for Mothering Sunday is furmety. This was a kind of caudle, made of whole boiled wheat, barley or oats, flavored and sweetened.

Furmety

Take 1 pt. of fine oatmeal and add to it 2 qts. of boiled water. Let it stand all night. In the morning stir it and strain it into a basin with 3 or 4 blades of mace

and a quartered nutmeg. Set it on the fire and keep stirring it, and let it boil a quarter of an hour. Then add 1 pt. of white wine, 3 teaspoons of orange-flower water, the juice of 2 lemons and 1 orange, a bit of butter and as much fine sugar as will sweeten it. Thicken with the yolks of 2 or 3 eggs.

Palm Sunday is also called Fig Sunday, and in Wales, Flowering Sunday or Carling Sunday. Sometimes home-brewed beer or cider was served at the church service, together with one large cake, of which the priest had the first slice. Later, small cakes were used in the place of the large one and on each cake was stamped the figure of the lamb and the flag, and each parishioner was given a cake as he left the service.

From Berkshire comes this jingle:

> "Beef and bacon's out of season,
> I want a pan to parch my peas on."

Carlings

Carlings are gray peas soaked in water and then fried in butter. Also known as parched peas, they are served in northern England on Palm or Carling Sunday, the fifth Sunday of Lent.

Bananas

In the Canary Islands the fruits are cut lengthwise, for when cut across they show the symbol of the crucifixion.

Figs

Figs grown in the garden of the Cistercian Convent in Rome, when cut through, reveal a green cross inlaid on white pulp.

On Fig Sunday (Palm Sunday), it was usual to eat figs, or fig pudding, at the midday dinner, and enormous quantities of the fruit were annually sold for the purpose. Figs were consumed while the parable of the barren fig tree was retold.

Fig Pudding

1 lb. chopped figs	½ cup sugar
1 cup suet, chopped	2 eggs
1 cup molasses	1 tsp. soda
¾ cup milk	3 cups pastry flour, sifted
¼ tsp. salt	

Mix ingredients, turn into greased mold or covered baking dish, and steam 5 hours. Serve with hot lemon sauce or whipped cream sweetened and flavored with rum or brandy.

To the Pennsylvania Dutch belongs the credit of bringing the custom of Green Thursday to America, and perpetuating it here for many generations. Everyone ate some fresh herbs and green vegetables during the day. Other racial groups followed the practice also, but not on so widespread a scale.

"Soon will come Green Thursday
When we shall bake the Lamb
We shall eat Judases farina
And three spoonfuls of honey."

Judases and honey are served at breakfast in Czechoslovakia. Judases are breakfast cakes of twisted dough, made to look like rope, suggesting the fate of Judas, the betrayer, who "went and hanged himself" in remorse, after he had identified Jesus to His enemies. Honey was believed to be a preventive against disaster, and a potent antidote against serpent stings.

As in Czechoslovakia, on Green Thursday the traditional Beránek (Easter Lamb Cake) is baked in America. In a large Czechoslovakian section of Texas one finds this recipe being used:

Beránek (Velikonočhí beránek—Easter Lamb Cake)

½ lb. confectioner's sugar
2 whole eggs
5 egg yolks
1 tsp. vanilla

Juice and rind of ½ lemon
1 bitter almond
5 egg whites beaten stiff
½ lb. allpurpose flour (it should be a little more, roughly 2 heaped cups)

The sugar, eggs (2) and yolks (5), vanilla, and lemon rind are beaten together by hand for 30 minutes (or an equivalent time with mixer). Then add the grated bitter almond and the lemon juice. Very slowly fold in, alternately, the stiffly beaten egg whites and the flour (sifted).

The utensil shaped like a lamb is buttered and sprinkled with bread crumbs. The cake mixture is then slowly poured into it and baked in a medium hot oven (375° for an hour). The lamb cake is allowed to cool before it is frosted.

Frosting

Beat 1 egg white with ¼ lb. confectioner's sugar and 1 tsp. lemon juice until the mixture thickens. Spread over the lamb cake. Add 2 raisins for eyes, and a sliver of a candied cherry for the mouth. When the frosting dries, tie a red ribbon around the lamb's neck.

Lamb Cake Variation (Not Frosted)

1 stick unsalted butter
¼ lb. sugar
4 egg yolks
Salt
Lemon rind

1 tsp. vanilla
1 cake yeast
1 lb. sifted allpurpose flour
1½ cups milk (about)
1-2 oz. blanched almonds (slivered)
1-2 oz. raisins

Cream the butter and add sugar, egg yolks, salt, lemon rind, and vanilla. Beat for 20 minutes. Then add the prepared yeast, sifted flour, and lukewarm milk (enough to prepare a medium heavy dough). Add the slivered blanched almonds and raisins and knead the dough thoroughly. Allow to rise. Prepare the lamb form as in the previous recipe, fill it with the prepared dough, and allow it to rise further in the form. Preheat the oven in the meantime, then close the form before baking.

Bake at 375° for an hour. (With some forms, the lamb cake should be turned over once to have it baked equally on both sides.) Cool the baked lamb cake and remove carefully from form. Immediately sprinkle it with confectioner's sugar, add raisins for eyes, tie a red ribbon around its neck, and place on a lace doily.

Not varying too greatly from the Czechoslovakian is the modern American version of the Lamb Cake, to be prepared in a mold that is available in most hardware stores:

Easter Lamb Cake

1 cup butter or margarine	¾ tsp. baking powder
1 cup sugar	½ tsp. salt
4 eggs (whole)	1 tsp. vanilla or grated rind of 1 lemon
2 cups allpurpose flour	

Cream butter, gradually adding sugar, beating until light and fluffy. Beat in eggs one at a time. Sift together flour, baking powder, and salt. Add to batter slowly and mix until blended. Add vanilla or grated lemon rind. Before filling lamb mold, coat both sides of mold with mixture of 2 tbsp. shortening blended with 1 tbsp. flour. Pour batter into face side of mold, filling it level with the top. Place spoonful of batter in center of other side of mold and some in ear tips. Place forms together, face side down, and set on baking sheet. Bake at 375° for an hour. To remove cake from mold, take off top lid and allow steam to escape. Let stand 10 to 15 minutes. Turn out on cake cooler. When cake is thoroughly cooled, cover with seven-minute frosting. Sprinkle lamb cake lightly with shredded coconut. Make face of raisins. Tie ribbon with bell around neck. Coconut tinted green serves as "grass."

Seven-Minute Frosting

2 egg whites (unbeaten)	5 tbsp. cold water
1½ cups sugar	2 tsp. light corn syrup
Salt	1 tsp. vanilla

Combine egg whites, sugar, dash of salt, water, and corn syrup in top of double boiler. Beat with egg beater about 2 minutes, or until thoroughly mixed. Cook over boiling water, beating constantly, about 5 minutes, until frosting stands in stiff peaks. Use rubber spatula to scrape bottom and sides of pan. Remove from boiling water. Add vanilla and beat. Makes 4 cups of frosting.

Good Friday is a day of mourning in many Christian churches in all lands. It was observed as the strictest fast day in the early church. Many superstitions surround this day, one being that water dipped before sunrise without a spoken word has healing power and will stay pure all year. In Macedonia no vinegar is used, for Christ was mocked with vinegar.

Bread baked on Good Friday, if hardened in the oven, could be kept all year, and its presence protected the house from fire. Sailors took loaves of it on their voyages to prevent shipwreck. In Florida, as late as 1879, three Good Friday loaves thrust into a heap of corn were considered sufficient to protect it from the ravages of rats, mice, and weevils. The commonest use of such bread or buns was a cure for diarrhea, dysentery, and a hundred other complaints. The bread was finely grated, mixed with milk or water, and given to the patient as a medicine.

The cross on the "hot cross buns" is believed by many to be a purely Christian emblem—it is, however, far older than the advent of Christianity. The cross was a pagan symbol long before it had any Holy Week significance. The first crosses appeared on cakes associated with the worship of Diana.

The little wheaten cakes that are known to have been made at primitive spring festivals were similarly marked. Two small loaves, each with a cross on it, were discovered under the ruins of Herculaneum, the city that was encased by volcanic ash in the year A.D. 79.

An English tale states that at an inn in London called the "Widow's Son," a bun is ceremonially laid in a basket containing many others by a sailor who receives free beer as his reward. In the early nineteenth century, the licensee of this inn was a widow. If her sailor son happened to be at sea on Good Friday, she laid aside, every year, a hot cross bun against the day of his return. One year he did not return, then, or ever again. The widow would not give up hope, and continued her practice of keeping a bun for him, hanging it up in the bar parlor until the next Good Friday came around, when she put it with the other accumulation of buns. After her death, later tenants followed the same custom, and now a clause in the lease enforces the custom. During World War II, the collection of buns was housed in a skittle alley under the bar to insure its safety during air raids. Many of the older buns are still in a state of perfect preservation, but some of those made with inferior flour during the two wars are already crumbling away.

Hot Cross Buns

1 cup milk, scalded	3 cups flour
½ cup sugar	½ tsp. cinnamon
3 tbsp. melted butter	½ cup currants
½ tsp. salt	1 tsp. grated lemon peel
1 yeast cake	1 pinch ground cloves
¼ cup warm water	Confectioner's sugar and milk
1 egg, well beaten	

Combine milk, sugar, butter, salt. When lukewarm, add yeast cake dissolved in water. Then add egg and mix well. Sift flour and cinnamon together, and stir into yeast mixture. Add currants, lemon peel, and cloves, and mix thoroughly. Cover and let rise in warm place until double in size. Shape dough into round buns and place on well-buttered baking sheet. Let rise again. Brush top of each bun with egg. Make a cross on each bun with a sharp knife. Bake in hot oven (400°) for 20 minutes. Remove from oven and brush over lightly with a cross made of confectioner's sugar moistened with milk.

On Good Friday, Czechoslovakian cooks prepare the Easter bread (coffee cake) which must not be cut or eaten until the priest says, "Christ is risen." That bread is always marked with a deep cross.

Mazanec (*A rich Czechoslovakian yeast bread*)

1 lb. allpurpose flour	1 tsp. vanilla
1¼ sticks unsalted butter	1 cake yeast
Pinch of salt	4 egg yolks
¼ lb. sugar (powdered)	1 cup milk
Grated lemon rind	¼ lb. raisins

¼ lb. almonds

Sift flour into a large bowl and cut the butter into the flour. Add salt, powdered sugar, lemon rind, vanilla. Put yeast to rise in a little bit of cream to which sugar has been added. Add to the flour mixture. Beat egg yolks slightly in the milk and add to the rest. Work the dough first in the bowl, then transfer to a board covered lightly with flour. The dough should be fairly heavy but must be kneaded thoroughly. Then add the raisins and the slivered blanched almonds, place the dough back into the bowl, cover with a clean napkin and let rise in a warm place for ¾ hour. At the end of that time the dough begins to rise, form into a round loaf and place on a buttered cookie sheet and allow to rise for another ¾ hour. Before placing into the oven, take a sharp knife and cut a cross on top of the loaf. Beat an egg and spread it all over the top. Let this dry and then repeat, this time covering the whole loaf with slivered almonds, which will stick to the egg and not fall off. Bake 1 hour.

Note: The proportions of the ingredients and the taste of this Easter bread are very much like the Russian "Kulich."

Good Friday Soup

For each person, in butter in a heavy stewpan, fry 1 sliced medium onion to a light brown. Add 1 tbsp. flour for each onion and stir with a wooden spoon over moderate heat until light brown. Add hot vegetable stock (1 cup for each person) and stir until soup is smooth and thick. Season to taste with pepper and salt. Place 3 or 4 very thin slices of cheese in the bottom of the tureen and pour the soup over them. Serve with dry toast.

In many Catholic countries throughout the world the Lenten fast is broken at midnight on Holy Saturday, and at that time the food for the Easter table is blessed. The Moravian church observes Easter in Bethlehem, Pennsylvania, and Winston-Salem, North Carolina, in a traditional manner. On Saturday afternoon a trombone choir plays from a church steeple, after which there is a "love feast." Later the choir meets in the belfry, and at midnight they go from house to house playing chorales, continuing until Easter morning. A traditional Moravian breakfast of sugar cake and coffee is served before the choir returns to the church for the service that precedes the sunrise.

Egg Toddy

In Sweden on Easter Eve a traditional egg toddy—a foamy drink made of spirits, boiling water, sugar and egg yolk—is passed around. The Swiss also drink their Äggtoddy, made in similar fashion.

Easter Day itself has many traditional menus, many of which are offered on American tables. Old England on Easter ate gammon (bacon) and the ham decreed by William the Conqueror. There was always a tansy pudding, described below. Often red herrings were arranged to resemble a man on horseback and placed in the center of a corn salad—this was a symbol of Christ's departure. Traditionally, Italians eat roast baby lamb, artichokes, and "Easter cakes." These are made of bread dough baked in huge rings or round loaves, frosted all over and covered with Jordan almonds or surrounded with candy eggs.

The Easter ham introduced by William the Conqueror (who wished to have a non-Semitic meat served) has become a traditional meat to be served in America as the main course of the Easter dinner. Whether sugar-cured or smoked or both, baked or boiled, its pink succulent coloring and its pleasing aroma make the Easter table a festive one.

In an 1804 London cook book, we find a recipe for tansy pudding, symbolic of the bitter herbs traditionally served at the Paschal Feast.

Tansy Pudding

To 4 Naples biscuits grated, put as much boiling hot cream as will wet them. Then beat up the yolks of 4 eggs, and have ready a few chopped tansy leaves, with as much spinach as will make it a pretty green. Be careful that you do not put in too much tansy, as that will make it bitter. When the cream be cold, mix all together with a little sugar and set it over a slow fire till it be thick. Then take it off and when cold put it in a cloth well buttered and floured. Tie it up close and let it boil three-quarters of an hour. Take it up in a basin, and let it stand one-quarter of an hour. Then turn it out carefully and put around it white wine sauce.

Or you may make a tansy pudding with almonds thus: Blanch 4 ounces of almonds and beat them very fine with rose-water. Pour a pint of cream boiling hot on a French roll sliced very thin. Beat 4 eggs well and mix with them a little sugar and nutmeg grated, a glass of brandy, a little juice of tansy and the juice of spinach to make it green. Put all the ingredients into a stew pan with a quarter of a pound of butter, and give it a gentle boil. You may either boil or bake it in a dish, lined with writing paper or with a crust.

Naples Biscuit (1)

A very old and very delicate recipe: 1 lb. pulverized sugar, 1 lb. sifted flour, 1 dozen eggs, a level teaspoonful of powdered mace. Beat yolks and whites separately. Add sugar to the yolks and beat well. Add whites and flour alternately, having put a pinch of salt and the mace into the flour. Bake about an inch-and-a-half thick in square pans in a moderate oven, increasing the heat until well done. Cut in bars and ice.

Icing, Boiled

Put 2 teacups granulated sugar and one-half of cold water to boil, stirring until the sugar is melted. Then do not stir until a drop in cold water will make a soft ball. Take off immediately, beat the whites of two eggs to a stiff froth and pour on the sugar, stirring all the while. Beat until stiff enough to spread. Flavor with vanilla.

Naples Biscuit (2)

1 lb. flour and 1 lb. sugar, 12 whites and 10 yolks of eggs. Beat the egg whites and yolks separately, as for other cakes. 2 glasses of wine. Naples should gradually harden in the oven, and be frequently turned in the tins.

Aside from other things, spring in Somerset County, Maryland, means that a few families at least enjoy tansy pudding, a confection made from the juice of the fresh young feathery shoots of the tansy plant. Tansy is a pungent, weedy herb that sports little yellow button-like flowers in terminal clusters in summer. This wayside plant was once cultivated in colonial gardens and used for a tonic and as a panacea for various ailments. How it ended up as tansy pudding (looking like hamburgers sprinkled with sugar) is not too well known.

Tansy Pudding (Maryland Variety)

¼ lb. butter	1 cup tansy juice
1½ pounds brown sugar	1 cup clover or wheat juice
10 eggs, separated	1 light pint of flour
1½ pts. milk	18 white-square crackers (rolled fine)
	½ tsp. salt

Cream butter and sugar. Separate eggs, adding yolks to mixture of butter and sugar. Add milk, tansy and wheat juices, flour, cracker crumbs, and salt. Fold in stiffly beaten egg whites. Cook mixture either as pancakes or pour batter into a hot greased "spider" (known as a frying pan to most people) and stir constantly so as not to brown. Cool—keep in tureen in refrigerator—when ready to serve make into cakes, brown and serve. Delicious!

If batter is used for pancake type of dessert, just pour on griddle; if for cooky type affair, scramble batter while cooking as you would for scrambled eggs.

Some people assert that the batter is delicious as a beverage without cooking, as the tansy juice gives it a peppermint flavor.

It has even been suggested that it be used as the basis for a springtime variation of eggnog.

Another Maryland custom that has a tie-in with Easter is the Hams and Eggs show which takes place in Upper Marlboro during the third week in March. Both the Maryland and United States Departments of Agriculture and the University of Maryland co-operate with local schools in staging the show, and prizes are given for the best home-cooked ham and home-grown eggs.

From the American-Czechs:

Crown Roast of Lamb

1 cup water	1½ cups finely chopped onion
½ cup butter or margarine	1 crown roast of lamb (5 lbs.)
1 pkg. (8 oz.) bread stuffing mix	Parsley sprigs
1 egg, beaten	Preserved kumquats
2 cups finely chopped celery	Cooked small white onions

Combine water and butter. To it add the packaged bread stuffing mix, the beaten egg, celery and chopped onion; mix well. Place lamb on rack in shallow roasting pan. Fill center of crown roast with stuffing mixture. Bake in a 325° oven for 2½ hours or until a meat thermometer registers 175° to 180°, depending on degree of doneness that is desired. Garnish lamb with parsley, kumquats, and small onions. Serves 8.

Bábovka is a round Czechoslovakian coffee bread served with hot coffee on Easter morning. It is generally baked in one of the round fluted cake forms with a hole in the middle. The word *bábovka* covers a wide variety of cakes ranging from yeast-risen "coffee-cake" breads to the pound cake variety. Some of the recipes are very similar to those for the *Mazanec* and for the first lamb cake recipe. There are at least thirteen recipes for *Bábovka*. This one is called

Bábovka si šlehanon smetanon (with whipped cream)

⅓ lb. confectioner's sugar
6 egg yolks
1 tsp. vanilla
Lemon rind
1 bitter almond

Juice from ½ lemon
6 egg whites beaten stiff
1 heaped cup sifted allpurpose flour
1¾ cup whipped cream (sweeten to taste)
Chocolate frosting

Beat the sugar, egg yolks, vanilla, lemon rind, and grated almond for 25 minutes by hand. Add lemon juice, a drop at a time. Then add alternately the stiffly beaten egg whites and the sifted flour. In the meantime, prepare the form, butter or flour it, and pour the dough in it. The *bábovka* should be baked in a moderately hot oven for ½ to ¾ hour. Allow to cool and take out gently. The next day, cut off the top (about ½ inch) of the *bábovka*. (By top here is meant the portion which is on top when baking, but actually the bottom of the finished cake.) Cut the slice carefully, because it will be used later and should remain whole. Now make a big hollow in the cake without letting the sides collapse. Fill the cake with sweetened whipped cream and cover with the top and reverse on a plate. (The top is now at the bottom.) Cover the cake quickly with chocolate frosting and place in refrigerator before serving.

Roast Lamb, Extraordinaire (From East Boston, Massachusetts)

1 leg of lamb, 5 to 6 lbs.
Soft butter
Salt and pepper
Paprika

1 large onion, sliced
2 large carrots, sliced
2 cups hot strong coffee
1 tbsp. sugar

1 tbsp. cream

It is optional whether to remove the parchment covering on the leg of lamb. Rub the leg of lamb with the soft butter and season by sprinkling with salt, pepper, and paprika. Make a bed of the onion and carrot slices on the rack on the bottom of the roasting pan. Then lay the roast on top of the vegetables. Roast uncovered in a preheated oven at 325°, allowing 20 minutes to a pound. Mix the two cups of hot strong coffee with sugar and cream; pour over leg of lamb ½ hour before the lamb is done. Baste frequently. Remove the lamb to a hot platter and place in turned-off oven to keep warm. Remove onions and carrots from pan; then remove excess fat. Make a gravy by placing the pan on top of the stove over a medium flame. While the liquid is simmering, scrape all the brown drippings clinging to the pan into the gravy, and stir. Serve in a warm bowl as an accompaniment to the roast. Serves 6.

Traditional since the Middle Ages, Italian Easter Pie has been considered a kind of cheese cake. Yet it differs from the fluffy variety known in America in that it has substantial texture. The crust, *Pasta Frolla,* is light, tender and similar to a rolled cooky dough. The two combine in this modern version of a favorite last course for the Easter feast.

Italian Easter Pie

7 tbsp. quick-cooking tapioca
¾ tsp. salt
2 cups milk
1 tbsp. sugar
½ tsp. ground cinnamon

Mix tapioca, ¼ tsp. salt, 1 tbsp. sugar, and ¼ tsp. cinnamon in a saucepan. Gradually stir in the milk. Cook to full boil (6 to 8 minutes), stirring. Remove from heat; cool 15 minutes. Stir well; chill. Next prepare: Pasta Frolla.

Pasta Frolla

1½ cups sifted flour
¾ tsp. baking powder
⅓ cup butter
⅓ cup sugar
½ tsp. grated lemon rind
4 eggs, separated
2½ cups creamed cottage cheese
2 tbsp. lemon juice
½ cup chopped mixed candied fruit

Meanwhile, sift together 1½ cups sifted flour, ¼ tsp. salt, and ¾ tsp. baking powder. Cream ⅓ cup butter; add ⅓ cup sugar and ½ tsp. grated lemon rind. Add 1 egg; beat well. Gradually stir in sifted dry ingredients; mix well. Reserve ⅓ of the Pasta; line a 9-inch spring-form pan with remaining ⅔. Press Pasta evenly over bottom and up sides of pan to within ½ inch of the top. Bake at 400° for 18 minutes. Beat the cottage cheese with a rotary beater until smooth. Add egg yolks one at a time, beating well after each addition. Add remaining ¼ tsp. salt, ¼ tsp. cinnamon, and lemon juice. Gradually add chilled tapioca mixture, blending. Fold in fruits, then the 4 stiffly beaten egg whites. Pour into cooled Pasta-lined pan. Roll the reserved Pasta on a lightly floured board to a 6x10-inch rectangle. Cut into 6 (10-inch long) strips. With these make a lattice top for the pie, folding strips over outside edges to seal. Bake at 350° for 80 minutes. Turn oven off; cool cake with door partly open for 1 hour. Chill before serving. Makes 12 servings.

We are indebted to the Friends of Greece in Boston for the following:

Mäyiritsä (Easter Soup)

Boil lamb bones for stock. Boil lamb heart and a piece of the lung till tender. Cut heart, lung, and meat of the bones into very small pieces. Add to lamb stock. Add finely chopped fresh onions and a little rice, salt and pepper. Let boil till rice is cooked. Remove from fire and add *avgolemono* (see recipe).

Avgolemono

Beat 2 eggs, add juice of lemon to taste. Slowly stir, a little bit at a time, 1 cup of the hot soup into egg mixture, stirring constantly. Then pour all this into the soup, while stirring. Cook for a few minutes over low fire, stirring the soup all the time.

Grecian Feast Bread

1 pkg. hot roll mix
¾ cup warm water
1 unbeaten egg
1 egg yolk
⅓ cup each raisins, chopped citron, candied cherries, chopped almonds
1 slightly beaten egg white
¾ cup sifted confectioner's sugar mixed with 1½ tbsp. cream

Sprinkle yeast from roll-mix package into ¾ cup warm water; dissolve; add an unbeaten egg, an egg yolk, and the dry mix. Let rise at 85° to 90° temperature until doubled in size, about 30 to 60 minutes. Turn out on floured surface and knead in raisins, candied cherries, citron, and almonds. Divide dough into three parts. Shape each into smooth ball and place on greased baking sheet 1 inch apart, in 3-leaf clover design. Let rise in warm place until doubled in size, again 30 to 60 minutes. Brush tops with beaten egg white. Bake at 375° for 25 to 30 minutes until golden brown. Glaze while still warm with confectioner's sugar combined with cream. Decorate with blanched almonds and candied cherries.

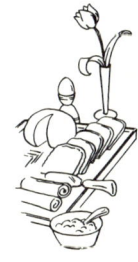

America has its own special contributions to the Easter festive board, and the following are some of the best of the many, many recipes prepared in the United States. From Virginia comes this recipe:

Baked Ham, "The Shepherds of Norfolk"

Choose a good Virginia ham weighing 8 or 9 lbs. Cover the ham with cold water and let it soak for 12 hours. Then cut away the rusty parts from the under side and edges. Scrub with a coarse cloth or stiff brush. Put on to boil in cold water, being sure that the ham is entirely covered with water all the time it is boiling. Allow a quarter of an hour for each pound the ham weighs, and let it boil slowly. Lift from pot, but do not remove the skin of the ham until it is completely cold. Wait until the day after it is boiled if possible. After skinning, wipe the ham dry and place it upside down in a baking dish. Cover the bottom of the baking dish with a paste made of 4 cups of brown sugar and 1 cup apple or peach brandy. Cook in the oven for 10 minutes at 350°, then take the dish out and turn the ham over and stick allspice all over the top and sides. Put back into the oven, and bake at 325°, basting continually until brown. It should take about half an hour. Serve with a tuft of fringed paper twisted about shank, and garnish the dish with parsley. Cut ham in very thin slices in serving.

There are many sauces that may be served with traditional Easter ham:

Cranberry-Raisin Sauce for Ham

½ cup brown sugar	⅛ tsp. dry mustard (pinch)
1 tbsp. cornstarch	1 cup cranberry juice cocktail
¼ tsp. ground cloves	1 tbsp. lemon juice
	2 tbsp. raisins

Mix sugar, cornstarch, clove, and mustard in a saucepan. Gradually stir in cranberry juice, lemon juice, and raisins. Cook over medium heat and stir until sauce is thick, about 5 to 7 minutes. Serve hot. Makes 1½ cups.

Mustard Sauce

⅛ tsp. pepper	1½ tsp. prepared mustard
½ tsp. salt	Lemon juice
	1 cup cream

Mix seasonings and lemon juice, gradually stirring in the cream. Combine well. Serve. Makes 1¼ cups.

Cider Sauce

½ cup raisins	¾ cup orange juice
2 cups cider	½ cup brown sugar
	¼ tsp. cloves

Plump the raisins by boiling them first, then drain and add to other ingredients. Simmer for 20 minutes and serve. Yield—2 cups.

Orange Sauce

3 tbsp. butter	¼ cup vinegar
4 tbsp. flour	¼ cup brown sugar
1 cup orange juice	2 tsp. grated orange peel
6 tbsp. sherry	2 tsp. crystallized ginger

Melt butter. Stir in flour until browned. Add balance of ingredients and cook over low heat for 15 minutes. Yield—1½ cups.

From Georgia:

Easter Blanc Mange

Save eggshells for several days before you wish to make this dish, being careful to open the eggs at one end, as small an opening as possible for the whites and yolks to slip out. Four cups of milk, whites of 3 eggs beaten, 3 tbsp. cornstarch, 4 tbsp. sugar, 1 tsp. lemon extract, 1 tbsp. gelatin. Soak the gelatin in just enough water to cover it. Dissolve the cornstarch in half the milk, add sugar and stiffly beaten whites of eggs. Let the rest of the milk come to a boil and then add gelatin and the mixture. Let it all come to a boil, and then when it has cooled a very little, enough for you to manage it easily, pour mixture into the eggshells. Have already prepared a bed of meal to set the eggs in, and set them aside to cool. This amount should fill 8 or 10 eggshells. When ready to serve, whip very stiff 2 cups of cream, color with green vegetable coloring matter, or any preferred color, spread cream on platter and lay in the eggs, after you have peeled off the shells. This dish can be made with many variations, such as making the eggs different colors, using a yellow custard in place of whipped cream, etc. It has been the delight of Southern children for many generations. If this dish is made for grown people, add one-half cup of blanched, finely chopped almonds to the blanc mange, and leave out the lemon. Serve with wine jelly laid around the eggs and less whipped cream.

From New York State:

Easter Eggnog Pie

1 envelope unflavored gelatin	¼ tsp. salt
¼ cup cold water	1 cup milk
2 eggs, separated	1½ tsp. rum extract
½ cup sugar	¼ tsp. nutmeg
½ cup heavy cream, whipped	

Soften gelatin in the cold water and set aside. Combine the two egg yolks, ¼ cup sugar, and the salt in a saucepan. Gradually stir in the milk. Cook over low heat until custard coats a metal spoon. Stir in softened gelatin, rum extract, and nutmeg.

Chill until mixture begins to thicken. Whip the cream and fold into mixture. Beat whites of eggs until they stand in soft peaks. Gradually add ¼ cup sugar and continue beating until stiff. Fold this into custard mixture and turn into a baked cooled pie shell (1 inch deep). Chill until firm and ready to serve, then garnish with a wreath of whipped cream if you wish, and arrange six mounds of green-tinted coconut on the wreath of whipped cream. Make a depression in each mound and fill with jellybean Easter eggs. Serves 6.

From Massachusetts:

Daffodil Cake

1 cup cake flour	½ tsp. vanilla extract
1½ cups sugar	½ tsp. almond extract
1⅓ cups egg whites	4 well-beaten egg yolks
¼ tsp. salt	2 tbsp. cake flour
1¼ tsp. cream of tartar	1 tsp. lemon extract

Sift 1 cup flour with ½ cup sugar 3 times. Beat egg whites until frothy; add salt and cream of tartar; beat until stiff but still glossy. Add 1 cup sugar a little at a time (sprinkle over egg whites); fold in thoroughly. Add vanilla and almond extracts. Sift flour mixture over top, a little at a time; fold in lightly with a down-over-up motion. Divide batter into 2 parts. Into one half fold egg yolks, 2 tbsp. flour, and lemon extract. Spoon batter alternately into 10-inch ungreased angel cake pan. Bake in moderate oven 325° for 1 hour. Invert pan to cool.

Cinnamon Rabbits

7 egg whites	2 cups pulverized almonds
2 cups granulated sugar	2 cups powdered sugar
5 tsp. cinnamon	Green sugar
1 lemon rind, grated	Currants

Beat the whites of the 7 eggs with the granulated sugar and the cinnamon until the mixture is stiff. Reserve one half of this mixture. To the other half add the grated rind of lemon, the almonds, and the powdered sugar. Knead this well and roll to a thickness of ½ inch. Cut into forms with a rabbit-shaped cutter. Then brush these with the remaining half of the mixture, sprinkle with green sugar, and add currants for the eyes. Bake until pale gold in color.

From Illinois:

Easter Bunnies

Use any deluxe roll recipe. Shape dough into long ropes ¾ to 1 inch in diameter, cut in 10- to 12-inch lengths. Tie in loose knots, bringing ends up straight to form ears. Press in raisins for eyes. Brush with diluted egg yolk. Let rise and bake as directed. While still warm, frost with confectioner's frosting; tint part of the frosting a delicate pink for the ears.

Easter Chick

Start with a shelled hard-cooked egg. Cut off a thin slice lengthwise to make a flat base. From another hard-cooked egg take the yolk, mash it and mix with mayon-

naise to make it soft and smooth. With a decorating tube filled with this mixture apply wings and head of chick. Insert a small bit of nut for the bill and a strip of pimiento for the comb. With a pointed knife make a small slit at the tail and insert a celery leaf or a small piece of curled endive. (To curl endive, cut the tip of a single leaf in parallel slits about an inch deep and soak in ice water.) Place the chick in a nest of watercress or shredded lettuce in the center of a salad platter, or use for individual salads.

From New York State:

Ice Cream Easter Bunnies

Use firm vanilla or Hawaiian pineapple orange ice cream. Use a large scoop for the body; a smaller scoop for the head. Place the two scoops one on top of the other and decorate with gumdrop sticks for ears, cinnamon drops for eyes, marshmallows for mouth and for tail. Hold in freezer until serving time, then line up on pastel-tinted coconut.

In Richmond, Maine, a refugee colony of 300 Russian families celebrates Easter a week after the western world's Easter, in a New World replica of an old Russian Orthodox Greek Catholic Church. The Orthodox Lent begins roughly eight weeks before Easter, and here in the United States, the Russian-Americans practice in freedom the age-old religion which they cherish so dearly. On Easter Eve, carrying icons, bright banners, censers, and the strangely shaped Easter foods, the parishioners file in procession to the church. There, after a ceremony of old Slavonic church songs and readings, the Easter foods are blessed. There is the tall cylinder-shaped *kulichi* (a rich coffee cake), the *pasha*, a pyramid-shaped cheese enriched with eggs, raisins and butter; there are fruits, preserves, honeycombs, meats, and many colorful Easter eggs. Many of the foods show the symbol XB (*Christos Voskresse*).

Russian Easter Cake (*Kulich*)

60 egg yolks	1 tsp. salt
6 cups sugar	½ lb. raisins
6½ tbsp. yeast (heaped tbsp.)	3 pc. cardamom
1 qt. milk	Nutmeg (½ of a whole one)
3 lbs. sweet unsalted butter	4 sticks vanilla rubbed with powdered
6½ lbs. allpurpose flour	sugar (or 1½ tsp. vanilla extract)

(A cup or two of diced citron or orange peel can be added if desired.) Cream egg yolks and sugar until the egg yolks turn lemon yellow. Dissolve the yeast in warm milk and when the yeast begins to rise, add to the egg-sugar mixture. Melt the butter and then cool it slightly before mixing it into the previous mixture. Add flour and salt slowly. Work the dough until it will no longer stick to your hands. With this quantity it is very hard work, but kneading should be done thoroughly to obtain best results. Work in the raisins, cardamom, nutmeg, and the vanilla sugar.

Prepare the form, which should be round and high. Line it with well-greased wax paper. Fill the form only to ⅓ or ½ full. Let the dough rise in the form. Bake when it begins to rise noticeably. All the ingredients that go into the *kulich* should be warm. The dough should, of course, be allowed to rise in a warm place. The baked *kulich* can be decorated with powdered sugar or with a white icing. Powdered sugar is mixed with 1 tbsp. of hot water and a little vinegar to get a good spreading consistency and should dry to a white glaze. This icing is put on after the cake has cooled.

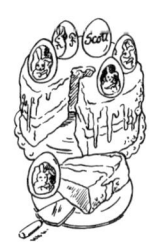

A little Austrian song extols the importance of foods at Easter time.

"We sing, we sing the Easter song;
God keep you healthy, sane and strong.
Sickness and storms and all other harm
Be far from folks and beast and farm,
Now give us eggs, green, blue and red;
If not, your chicks will all drop dead."

According to Hasting's *Dictionary of Christ and the Gospels,* it is generally believed that the Last Supper may not have coincided with the Passover, but that it probably was like a Paschal meal. The Lord's Supper was instituted by Jesus as a perpetual memorial to His death, and has been observed ever since by many Christians on Holy Thursday.

Feasting still continues through the Eastertide until Whitsun. The most popular of the Whitsuntide's food is the cheese tart, of which Ben Franklin was especially fond. Also appearing on that day's festive board are roast veal, baked custard, gooseberry pudding, plum cake, and ale. In Lancashire, England, a frosted muffin called the "topcake" is added to this starchy, rich array of foods.

In *Setting for Passover,* by Prudence Penny, we learn that the traditional table is set with symbolic foods and that the stirring story of the Exodus of the children of Israel from Egypt is read from the *Haggadah* (the "Bible" of the Jewish people). The Jewish people relive their ancestors' dramatic flight from Egyptian bondage. Although Passover deprives Jewish homemakers of certain everyday foods, it is still possible to serve well-balanced and easily prepared meals. To simplify holiday cooking, many new traditional Passover foods are now available in quick and convenient packaged form.

In front of the head of the house (who reads and recites the *Haggadah,* story of the Passover), the following are placed, either on a Seder plate or on a group of small plates:

Three whole matzoth—covered or inserted into the matzoth dish. A piece of the middle one (the Afikomen) is hidden for a child to find. A *roasted lamb bone*—to the right—to commemorate the sacrifice made by the Israelites in Egypt before leaving for the Promised Land.

A *roasted egg* is placed to the left of the host in mourning for the destroyed Temple.

Moror or *bitter herbs* (radish, horseradish, onions, scallions)—in the center—as a reminder of the bitterness of Israel's slavery in Egypt.

Charoseth (chopped almonds, grated apple, wine, sugar, and cinnamon)—

to symbolize the mortar with which the Jews were forced to lay bricks for Pharaoh.

Karpas (celery, parsley, any greens)—which means 600,000 in Hebrew, the number of Israelites that left Egypt.

Salt water—symbolizing the Red Sea that parted miraculously to let the Israelites escape.

Elijah Cup—traditionally a precious item filled with wine, is placed on the Seder table to await the beloved Prophet.

The Seder is traditionally begun by dipping a hard-boiled egg in salt water. As an alternative, a tasteful appetizer is "gefillte" eggs.

"*Gefillte*" *Eggs*

¼ cup minced onion
2 tbsp. Rokeach Nyafat
⅛ tsp. pepper
4 hard-cooked eggs
¼ tsp. salt

Sauté the minced onion in Nyafat (seasoned fat) until golden brown. Meanwhile, cut eggs in half from tip to tip. Remove and mash yolks. Add browned onions, any melted fat in skillet, and seasonings. Blend well. Pile seasoned yolks back into egg whites. Serve on lettuce as first course, as salad, or as an hors d'oeuvre.

Passover "*Rolls*"

½ cup seasoned fat
1 cup boiling water
2 cups matzoth meal
1 tbsp. sugar
1 tsp. salt
4 eggs

Add the seasoned fat to the boiling water in a saucepan and heat until the fat is melted. Add the dry ingredients all at once and beat rapidly, over low heat, until the mixture leaves the sides of the pan and forms a ball. Remove from heat and beat in eggs one at a time. Beat hard after each addition of egg until batter is thick, smooth. Shape into 8 balls. Place these on a well-greased baking sheet. Using the tip of paring knife, cut a roll design on top of each round. Bake in a moderate oven (375° F.) 1 hour or until golden brown.

8
The Easter Egg

Of all the folk symbols of Easter known to young and old, none is more conspicuous than the egg. To most of us, it is an even more familiar example of the beginning of life than the seed of a plant. However, the place of the egg in Christian tradition and folk observance is only a part of a fabulous story.

From the mythology of ancient Egypt and India we learn that the egg was a symbol of the creation of the world. These beginnings were associated with Geb, whose body was the earth, and Nut, the queen, who was the sky. The son of this union was Osiris, lord of the underworld. These two also produced an egg from which the universe developed. From this egg came the extraordinary Bennu bird or Phoenix, symbol of the sun. The early Christians adopted this bird as a representation or symbol of Christ, the Saviour. The phoenix was chosen for the belief that it died and came to life again. This feat was accomplished by the bird, which set fire to its nest and burned itself to ashes. In the ashes was an egg, which hatched to produce the destroyed bird. This strange event, it was believed, took place every five hundred years. In religious art, the phoenix resembles the peacock, another symbol of Christ's Resurrection.

Also of Egyptian origin is the story of Ptah, chief of the gods, who fashioned a golden egg at a potter's wheel while seated on his throne. He is described as "Father of beginnings, and creator of the egg of Sun and Moon."

From ancient Hindu culture we learn of the World-Egg (often referred to as the Mundane Egg), which was formed in the "waters of chaos" before time began. This was also a golden egg from which Prajapati, the father of all creatures, came forth. Another version of similar origin credits this god as the creator of the World-Egg, formed from his own perspiration. This egg also con-

tained both heaven and earth. In his book, *Easter, Its Story and Meaning,* Alan W. Watts quotes a Hindu scripture: "In the beginning of this world was merely non-being. It was existent. It developed. It turned into an egg. It lay for a period of a year. It was split asunder. One of the two eggshell parts became silver, one gold. That which was of silver is the earth. That which was of gold is the sky. What was the outer membrane is the mountains. What was the inner membrane is cloud and mist. What were the veins are the rivers. What was the fluid within is the ocean. Now, what was born therefrom is yonder sun."

Old Phoenician culture has given us a similar story of the origin of the egg from water.

These wondrous accounts seem remote, in a way, from the brightly colored egg trees of German origin, the delightful customs of Christian Europe and parts of Asia, the egg-rolling contests in the nation's capital, and the delectable candy eggs and similar confections of our own day. And yet, the egg as a symbol of death and life has been apparent to practically every race down through the ages. The shell may well be compared to a tomb which encases a germ of life. When the shell is broken or disintegrated, a new life is born.

It was Thomas Aquinas, the great theologian of the thirteenth century, who posed the riddle, "Which came the first, egg or hen?" The preponderance of the argument indicated that the hen came first. The great religionist wrote that "every imperfect thing must needs be preceded by some perfect thing: for seed is from some animal or plant." The ancient myths of Egypt and India were based on the same reasoning. Geb was referred to as "the Great Cackler" or Gander. Hamsa the divine swan, a symbol of Brahma, was often portrayed in Hindu art floating on the waters of chaos with the World-Egg beneath him. In *Easter, Its Story and Meaning,* Alan Watts states, "In the Finnish epic known as the 'Kalevala,' by Elias Lönnrot, the earth, sky, sun, moon and clouds are said to have been formed from the broken eggs of a teal sent by Ukko, the highest god, to nest upon the knee of the Water-Mother."

The Hawaiians believe that the large island of Hawaii was produced by the bursting of an egg that had been laid on the water by a bird of great size, and that there was no other land. Did not the instinct of our own forefathers, too, give utterance to this oracle, "Everything springs from the egg, it is the world's cradle"?

In Hutchinson's *History of Northumberland* we read that the Jewish people adopted the Egyptian concept of the egg "to suit the circumstances of their history, as a type of their departure from the land of Egypt; and it was used in the feast of the Passover . . . The eggs were boiled until hard and served as symbols of a bird called Ziz, a storied creature in Hebrew tradition."

In medieval days, the curious symbol of the World-Egg appears in the work of the alchemists. Strange performers and dabblers, these men were seeking to do many things that smacked of superstition and occult practices. One of their aims was to transform lead into gold. Curiously enough, the vessel used was called the aludel and shaped like an egg. This was placed in a furnace which served as a kind of incubator to hatch the philosopher's stone that would change lead to gold by merely touching the earthly metal. Drawings of the period indicate the presence of a bird which appeared to be a composite of a phoenix, a gander, and a pelican.

Again, we have a link with Thomas Aquinas, since the pelican was associated with Christ in the folk mind, for it was believed that this bird fed its young with its own blood. A prayer of this Italian theologian describes the belief: "Pelican of mercy, Jesu, Lord and God, cleanse me, wretched sinner, in thy precious Blood; Blood, whereof one drop for humankind outpoured, Might from all transgression have the world restored."

If the resurrection of the body had been a tenet of the ancient Egyptians, undoubtedly they would have thought an egg to be a highly important symbol. The emergence of a living creature by incubation after a long period of dormancy is a process so truly marvelous that, if it could be disbelieved, it would be thought by some a thing as incredible as that the author of life should be able to reanimate the dead.

The links between these ancient myths and the use of eggs in Christian tradition are not easily traced. Early missionaries, or the knights of the Crusades, may have been the bearers of the egg tradition, which assumed significance at an early date in the Christian era. Surely, no more fitting symbol could be used to teach the story of the Resurrection than an egg.

"We beseech thee, O Lord, to bestow thy benign blessings upon these eggs, to make them a wholesome food for thy faithful, who gratefully partake of them in honor of the Resurrection of our Lord Jesus Christ." This is the prayer offered by Roman Catholic priests in various countries of Europe when eggs to be given as gifts are brought to the church. In *The Easter Book,* Francis X. Weiser reminds us that the egg was a symbol of the "rock tomb out of which Christ emerged to the new life of His Resurrection."

It was the custom in Europe for families to send great containers of hard-boiled eggs to the church to be blessed. The priest, after having finished the ceremony, used to inquire how many dozen each container held. Gifts of eggs were made to the clergy by children. These blessed eggs had the virtue of sanctifying the stomach, since they were the first fat or fleshy nourishment eaten after the abstinence of Lent. As soon as the eggs were blessed, they were carried home, and a large table was set in the best room in the house. The container of eggs was placed in the middle, surrounded by an elaborate array of meat on platters. In the great manor houses, the egg feast was further embellished with side tables displaying fine silver, pewter, and Delft ware, "in honour to their Easter eggs." These made a gala display, for the shells were painted with various colors and some were gilded. Often as many as twenty dozen were arranged in a large bowl, neatly laid together in the form of a pyramid. This elaborate setup was kept on display all through the Easter week, and all who came to visit were invited to eat an Easter egg. No one refused this repast, for the taste of an egg was good after the long Lenten fast.

Eggs as gifts were popular among the ancient Persians at the spring equinox, which was the beginning of their new year. As with all races, they looked forward to the renewal of all things each spring. Similarly, the Christians welcomed spring with its renewal of hope manifested by the death and Resurrection of the Saviour. In China, pickled eggs, often preserved for many years, were offered as gifts of special significance to distinguished visitors who came to call. The proper way to say thanks was to devour the egg, regardless of its age. Henry VIII received a Paschal egg in a case of silver filigree from the Vatican.

Among the early Christians of Mesopotamia, the children used to buy as many eggs as they could obtain, and stain them red in memory of the blood of Christ, shed at the Crucifixion. Green and yellow were other popular colors. Stained eggs were commonly sold in the markets. An enjoyable sport consisted of children striking their eggs, one against another. A similar custom describing the game of pace-egging indicates its popularity in the British Isles. "The majority of pace eggs are simply dyed, or dotted with tallow, to present a pie-bald or bird's eye appearance. These are designed for the junior boys. In the process of dyeing they are boiled pretty hard, so as to prevent inconvenience if crushed in the hand or the pocket. But the strength of the shell constitutes the chief glory of the pace egg, whose owner aspires only to the conquest over a rival youth. Holding his egg in his hand, he challenges his companion to give blow for blow. One of the eggs is sure to be broken, and its shattered remains are the spoil of the conqueror, who is instantly invested with the title of 'a cock of one, two, three,' etc., in proportion as it may have fractured his antagonists' eggs in the conflict. A successful egg, in the contest with one which had previously gained honours, adds to its number the reckoning of its vanquished foe. An egg which is a 'cock' of ten or a dozen is frequently challenged." This game is still played in many countries.

Colored eggs have special significance, as do the symbols with which they are decorated. Among the Greeks and the Syrians, crimson eggs were exchanged to represent the blood of Christ. Green was a favorite color in Germany and Austria for use on Maundy Thursday, and it was also the day on which green vegetables, such as dandelions, were gathered and cooked. The delicate tracery of ferns and other plants was used to ornament eggs in Austria by fastening the leaves around the eggs before they were cooked.

Among the Poles and the Ukranians, the art of decorating eggs involves unusual skill and imagination. Melted beeswax is applied before dyeing, and the process repeated as the eggs are dipped in various colors. These "designed" eggs are known as *pysanki,* and each is original in its design. They are blessed by the parish priest before they are presented to friends, and many are kept as cherished heirlooms. Symbols like the sun for good fortune, the rooster for fulfillment of wishes, the stag or deer for good health, and flowers for love convey the intended message.

With Yugoslavian families, markings and decorations on Easter eggs included

the letters "XV" for *Christos Vaskvese* (Christ is risen). Fish, crosses, and other religious symbols were characteristic of eggs decorated in Poland. Girls used to give their favorite admirers quantities of eggs which they had decorated themselves or obtained from women of the village who specialized in the art. Wrapped in an embroidered scarf or kerchief, they were offered with a small gift of suitable nature. When the recipient was serious in his intentions, he responded with a handsome gift of wearing apparel. In Armenia, the decorated eggs were adorned with pictures of the risen Christ, the Virgin Mary, or some other appropriate religious insignia.

In Germany, folklore is rich with stories about eggs. Sometimes instead of eggs at Easter, an emblematical print was presented. One of these is preserved in the Print-Room of the British Museum. Three hens are shown upholding a basket in which are placed three eggs ornamented with representations illustrative of the Resurrection. Over the center egg is the Agnus Dei (or Lamb of God), with a chalice representing faith; the other eggs bear the emblems of hope and of charity. Beneath all are the following lines:

> "All good things are three,
> Therefore I present you three Easter Eggs:
> Faith and Hope together with Charity.
> Never lose from the Heart
> Faith to the Church; Hope in God,
> And love Him to thy death."

A nineteenth-century traveler writing of German Easter customs observed that "Easter is another season for the interchange of civilities, when instead of the coloured egg in other parts of Germany, and which is there merely a toy for children, the Vienna Easter egg is composed of silver, mother-of-pearl, bronze, or some other expensive material, and filled with jewels, trinkets, or ducats."

One of the old stories told about an Easter observance concerns Edward I, who was king of England in the year 1290. The expense book of his household reveals that for 18 pence he purchased 450 eggs, which were colored or covered with gold leaf. These eggs were distributed to members of the royal household.

In parts of rural Europe, children used to ask for "paste eggs" as they went from door to door. They dressed in fancy or weird costumes, carried wooden swords, and blackened their faces or wore masks. Sometimes animal skins were used for the disguise, and the youngsters performed all the antics that their audiences would take. "Paste is a corruption of the ancient *pasche,* by which Easter is best known in many parts of Europe. Beggars used to plead for eggs also, and were seldom refused." In England as elsewhere, present-day children who go calling at Easter do not always receive colored eggs according to the old tradition, for this means special preparation. Rather candy eggs, cookies, and other sweets as well as coins have replaced the old-time hard-cooked eggs.

 The Easter egg tree, in many ways the counterpart of the Christmas tree, has become a fairly recent tradition in America, because of the wide-spread popularity of Katherine Milhous' delightful children's book, *The Egg Tree*. This custom of decorating evergreens or leafless trees with colored eggs, a novelty among the Pennsylvania Dutch, had its origin in the years following the Civil War. The older practice of suspending or impaling eggs in their natural colors on bushes and small trees outdoors was a custom of earlier date. Of German origin, this fashion was vividly portrayed in the color lithographs circulated in this country before the turn of the century. It was also practiced in other northern European countries.

Making such a tree requires considerable skill to obtain perfect shells for painting. Eggs to be used for the great Easter feast were not broken, but carefully punctured with a needle at both ends, and the contents blown into a bowl. Then the shells were ready to be painted or dyed, or otherwise decorated, and placed on the tree. An article which appeared in *Lothrop's Annual,* 1895, tells the story.

"The Easter-tree is a delightful feature of the Easter season in Germany. It is not so universal as the Christmas-tree; for in Germany there is no household so poor but the Christmas-tree finds a place in it, even though its branches may spread scarcely wider than the flowers of a good-sized bouquet. The Easter-tree is more common in northwestern Germany than elsewhere, and the tree-frolic is something all young people ought to know about.

"For an Easter party, at which the frolic is to take place, a large tree, set upon a good-sized table, stands in the center of the room. The larger the room the better. The tree is hung with *Oster Eier* (Easter eggs) of every color and size. During the year the children gather many varieties of birds' eggs and save them for decorating the Easter-tree. Hens, geese and turkeys' eggs are also colored by boiling them in solution of dye-stuffs—a strong one to make the deep colors, a weak one for the more delicate shades.

"Loops of bright-colored ribbons, always of contrasting shades, are pasted upon the eggs to hang them by, tip downwards. Tinsel ornaments and pendants; curious sugar people, cake animals, especially lambs and rabbits; Easter hens, and chickens; and dainty chocolate and sugar confections of every conceivable variety are fastened to the boughs, while underneath, upon the table or pedestal, sitting in special state the wonderful Easter rabbit, or sometimes the Easter lamb, presides over the gifts and favors concealed in the *Oster Hase's* nest."

In Germany it was often the practice to gild eggshells, fill them with candy and suspend them on ribbons. Decorated trees were often used in spring festival parades during the Easter season. Among the natives of the Virgin Islands, the fashion of placing decorated eggshells on the spiny stems of yucca plants was a practice of long standing. Decorated eggs, sometimes gilded, sometimes decorated like a globe to represent the world or elaborately ornamented with decalcomanias, used to be popular for decorating Christmas trees in various parts of Germany. Occasionally these are seen in America.

Another curious form of egg decoration formerly seen in Pennsylvania Dutch homes was the Easter egg bird. These were decorated shells in which four holes were made, one for the head, two for the wings, and one for the tail, plus an opening for attaching the bird to a thread so that it could be hung. These were popular a century ago and lasted indefinitely if not roughly handled.

As early as 1789, Easter eggs were ornately decorated with scratch-carving by the Pennsylvania Dutch. A sharp knife or some pointed tool was used to scratch the dyed surface of the egg. Considerable effort was put into making the design, and these eggs were often inscribed as presentation pieces. Naturally, they were cherished as keepsakes, and some have been kept for a hundred years or more. Typical Pennsylvania Dutch folk art designs including tulips, distelfinks, flat hearts, butterflies, and elephants were used. This craft was also popular in Germany and Switzerland. Scratch-carved eggs were obviously popular in Switzerland in the 1880's for there are interesting accounts of such eggs brought to Pennsylvania at that time.

Binsa-graws was a name familiar to those who decorated eggs with the pith of a meadow rush found in low ground. The woolly pith was forced out of the rush with a match and wound around the egg surface with a paste made of flour and water. Then pieces of brightly colored calico cut in a variety of shapes were added for further embellishment.

Onion skins were used to color the eggs. For yellow effects, alder catkins and hickory bark did the job. Madder root produced light red, and coffee and walnut shells made brown tones. Eggs wrapped tightly in calico made it possible to transfer patterns easily.

In nineteenth-century Pennsylvania men and children used to challenge each other as to who could eat the most eggs, as their forebears along the Rhine had done for generations. "Picking eggs" on Easter Sunday and Monday was the name used by children, who tested the strength of the shells by striking the ends together. The broken egg was the prize for the fellow who broke it. The custom is of ancient origin and is enjoyed as well in far-off Syria, Iran, and Iraq, and in various parts of Europe.

Another sport popular in Europe and America is rolling hard-boiled eggs against each other or downhill. The child who retains the last uncracked egg is the winner. This pleasant pastime has been observed on the lawn of the White House in Washington since the Presidency of James Madison, and many fascinating stories about this custom have been written. In 1922, Robert Shackleton in his *Book of Washington* recorded his impressions of this colorful event.

"The children gather by thousands, boys and girls, and all young. No adults are admitted, except such as are in definite charge of a child. What may be termed the childless fathers of Washington (not the fatherless children) form a long unbroken line, along the stone base of the enclosing iron fence, standing tiptoe and eager to watch the gay scene within. I took my chance with the general public, and was curtly refused admission by a particularly stern policeman whom I had noticed turning back one adult after another. I briefly said a half

dozen words to the effect that I was a stranger in the city, who had not brought a child. Apparently he did not hear me. He looked sternly over my shoulder at the Washington Monument, and in a growling undertone responded to 'go back a little and adopt a child.' So within five minutes I was within the grounds —and it was astonishing how soon that adopted boy was lost!

"The sweeping grounds were thronged. Every moment more were arriving. They came in singles and twos and threes and they came in a succession of little throngs as street car after street car unloaded; they came, very many, in motor cars. And in the closed cars the little children, gathered half a dozen or so in a car, looked like crowded nests of brightly plumaged birds, for it was a gathering that included every class. The rich and the well-to-do were there; the poor were there, proud of their colored eggs.

"There was no formal procedure. Each child carried its eggs, all fancifully decorated, and most of them sat quietly on the grass on knolls where their eggs rolled easily.

"There was, oddly, a general appearance as if there were only children, for the elders were practically lost, practically unnoticeable, among the gayly colored throng of little ones. Quite amazingly colorful were the children and their accessories: their parasols, their many-colored toy balloons, held by strings, the bright baskets, the eggs themselves, the hair ribbons, the jackets and hats and skirts, in reds and blues and lavenders, in mustards and pinks—there were children like lilies, all in white, children in pale linen, children like yellow daffodils, seated on the pale green grass.

"Some were moving about in gentle happiness. A great fountain was gloriously playing and all the lilacs were in delicate flower. Intermittently came the music of the Marine Band; and always was the softly chirring sound of children's voices.

"It makes the most picturesque scene in America, with its noble background of the White House: it was like some unusually beautiful fête day for children in France, with the beauty of grass and shrubs and trees and costumes accented by the noble jet d'eau."

The game proved to be so rough on the grass that the location of the festival was changed from the White House to the Capitol terraces. In the days before the Civil War, this custom was preceded by Sunday-school picnics and Easter parades. Another game consisted in throwing colored eggs into the air, like balls. The game ended when the last egg was broken.

Following World War II, an annual Easter Egg Rolling Contest, inaugurated by Arnold Constable and the Department of Parks, has been held in New York's Central Park. Wooden eggs are rolled, using wooden spoons, within a prescribed area across the lawn, by children from five to twelve. Prizes include popular toys and cash awards.

According to an old tale, in the days of the Crusades, egg rolling became a test for young knights who wanted to make the arduous journey in search of the Holy Grail. The winner of the contest proved his fitness.

Hunting for eggs in the house and in the garden has been a widespread practice on both sides of the Atlantic for generations. In Europe, notably in France, the children are told that the eggs are dropped by the bells on their return from Rome. This allusion relates to the bells of the Catholic Mass, which are silenced on Thursday of Passion Week, wooden clappers being used in their place. When the silencing of the bells occurs, people say that they have gone to Rome.

When the Easter fires are kindled in Fredericksburg, Texas, each year, the children are told that the celebration signifies the rabbits burning flowers to make the dyes for coloring the Easter eggs.

In Provence it has long been the custom to present an egg to a newborn child, together with bread, salt, and a knitting needle. The wish is that the child will be whole as an egg (endowed with all his faculties), good as bread, sharp as salt, and straight as a needle.

In Scotland, and in the north of England generally, it has long been customary to give children hard-boiled eggs as toys on Easter Sunday, presumably with the wish that the child will have a long life. Collecting duck and goose eggs has long been a favorite pastime with children in the Irish countryside. Prior to Palm Sunday, they make nests of stones in out-of-the-way places, and during Holy Week they gather the eggs to place in these nests. At Easter, the eggs are given to other youngsters whose families do not keep poultry, but each gatherer manages to eat his share. Parents give eggs as presents at Easter, particularly duck eggs.

An Englishman traveling in Greece gave the following account of Easter observance in Greece. "A small bier, prettily decked with orange and citron buds, jasmine, other flowers, and boughs, was placed in the church, with a Christ crucified, rudely painted on board, for the body. We saw it in the evening, and, before daybreak, were suddenly awakened by the blaze and crackling of a large bonfire, with singing and shouting, in honour of the Resurrection. They made us presents of colored eggs and cakes of Easter bread."

Easter Day, wrote the Abbé d'Auteroche, in his *Journey to Siberia,* written in the late eighteenth century, was set apart for visiting in Russia. "A Russian came into my room, offered me his hand, and gave me, at the same time, an egg. Another followed, who also embraced, and gave me an egg. I gave him, in return, the egg which I had just before received. The men go to each other's houses in the morning, and introduce themselves by saying, 'Jesus Christ is risen.' The answer is, 'Yes, He is risen.' The people then embrace, give each other eggs, and drink brandy." Eggs were colored red with Brazil wood, and it was the custom for each parishioner to present one to the parish priest on Easter morning. They were also carried for several days following Easter. Those of high station usually displayed gilded eggs and greetings and eggs were exchanged in the home, in the market place or on the road, wherever friends met.

On Easter morning in Russia, in the Ukraine, and in Poland, the egg plays a significant part in the beginning of a joyful day. Before breakfast is served, the father of the household cuts an egg that has been previously blessed and dis-

tributes pieces to all the members of his family, wishing them a happy and holy Easter. Then the family sits down to a hearty breakfast with eggs aplenty.

"Nothing," observes Kohl, a nineteenth-century writer on customs and manners, in his book *Russia*, "is more amusing than to visit the markets and stalls where the painted eggs are sold. Some are painted in a variety of patterns; some have verses inscribed on them, but the more usual inscription is the general Easter greeting, 'Christohs voskress'—'Christ is risen'; or 'Eat and think of me,' etc. The wealthier do not, of course, content themselves with veritable eggs, dyed with Brazil wood, but profit by the custom to show their taste and gallantry. Scarcely any material is to be named that is not made into Easter eggs. At the imperial glass-cutting manufactory we saw two halls filled with workmen, employed in nothing else but in cutting flowers and figures on eggs of crystal. Part of them were for the Emperor and Empress to give away as presents to the courtiers."

The Easter egg tradition is deeply rooted in Russian culture and in no country in the world has the egg been glorified in a more creative and enduring manner than by Carl Fabergé, the great goldsmith and jeweler of the late nineteenth and early twentieth centuries. Fabergé eggs are perhaps the most sought-after jewels of the Easter tradition in the twentieth century. They are often illustrated in newspapers and magazines, and in the spring of 1961 an exhibition of "Easter Eggs and Other Precious Objects" by Carl Fabergé held at the Corcoran Art Gallery in Washington, D.C., attracted international attention among art lovers and all who enjoy distinguished craftsmanship, so seldom seen in our machine age.

In the Catalog of the Exhibition, A. Kenneth Snowman, noted English authority on Fabergé, wrote: "Social historians of the future may well wonder how it was that, in the years following the second great World War, the popularity of certain precious objects designed and made by a pre-Revolution Russian craftsman should have increased and spread so prodigiously. The answer is not far to seek. Carl Gustavovitch Fabergé's philosophy was a simple and uncompromising one summed up in the word 'quality.' It has been said that as much as twenty per cent of his firm's output never left the St. Petersburg workshops where close to two hundred craftsmen worked. Every single article was submitted to Carl Fabergé before completion, for his approval, and, if he felt that the work fell short in any respect of the exacting standard he had set, it had to be scrapped and restarted."

Of French Huguenot extraction, the Fabergé family left their homeland in the seventeenth century and moved to Russia to escape persecution in their own land. It was in St. Petersburg that Peter Carl was born, in 1846. Four years earlier, his father, Gustav, a goldsmith and jeweler, had established a small business in a basement. After study in Europe, young Carl returned to St. Petersburg to find that his father's jewelry business was thriving. He was in a position to supply jewelry and precious objects of art to members of Russian royal families, and they were eager for his output.

The young craftsman set forth the standard that "in the matter of objects of *vertu* and jewels generally, the emphasis previously placed squarely on sheer value should be shifted to craftsmanship. The sincerity of a gift was to be measured rather by the amount of imagination shown in its conception than by a noisy demonstration of wealth. So he switched from the production of conventional articles of jewelry to the designing of decorative objects composed of materials of considerable beauty, but of no great intrinsic value."

The tzar became one of his chief patrons and each year Fabergé designed the fabulous jeweled Easter eggs, contrived with the utmost skill and imagination, which contained ingenious surprises. These were presented to the tzarina as gifts by her husband. The English Prince Consort, Albert, was another of Fabergé's patrons, who commissioned carvings in various semi-precious stones depicting many of the domestic animals at Sandringham. Fabergé was as adept in selecting suitable materials for his pieces as he was in choosing a particular craftsman to execute his design. He assembled craftsmen from Russia, Finland, Sweden, Germany, and other countries, and was able, by his own extraordinary skill, to inspire his men to create masterpieces which were first and foremost of distinction and true originality. Great artist that he was, Carl Fabergé had the ability to train each new craftsman to share the joy and the responsibility involved in his craft.

For his precious stones, Fabergé had the vivid Siberian emerald, the gray jasper of Kalgan, and the abundant mineral deposits found in the Urals, the Caucasus, Siberia, and elsewhere in Russia, from which to draw. Here was a truly great artist and craftsman who chose the right location for his business and assembled the best available skills to produce, for a receptive public, work of incomparable beauty. But it all came to an end with the outbreak of the First World War in 1914. "When the Communists took over control of private business houses, Fabergé is said to have asked, with a characteristic absence of ceremony, for ten minutes' grace 'to put on my hat and coat.' He died in Lausanne in 1920, an exile both from his country and his work."

Superstitions about eggs that have a way of turning up on occasion are not without interest. Eggs laid on Good Friday are believed to stay fresh indefinitely and, if kept, will insure success with poultry. An old French belief was that Good Friday eggs should be preserved all year so they could be used to extinguish fires when thrown on them. In the Balkan countries, painted eggs are thought to keep a house from evil. Planted in the ground, they protect the vines from the rigors of the elements. Fortunate is the farmer whose hen lays an egg on the roof of the house on Ascension Day, for his dwelling will be safe from harm. Dalmatians were careful to throw eggshells as far from the house as they could, to make a boundary line that snakes could not pass. Germans burned their eggshells because witches, who ordinarily could not cross water, could do so in eggshell boats.

Eggs laid on Good Friday and eaten on that day or on Easter Sunday insured good fortune and were used in folk medicine by the Pennsylvania Dutch to cure

many ailments. No sensible farmer would sell eggs laid on this day, for it meant parting with good fortune. These and many other interesting folk beliefs are included in *Eastertide in Pennsylvania,* by Alfred L. Shoemaker, published by the Pennsylvania Folklife Society at Kutztown, Pennsylvania.

Like the Christmas tree, the Easter rabbit is one of several notable contributions to American folklore made by the Pennsylvania Dutch. All across this broad land, it is the Easter rabbit or bunny who is supposed to bring the Easter eggs and other confections as well as the wide variety of gifts that attend the celebration of the greatest of spring holidays.

This fascinating custom introduced by the German settlers who began to arrive here in the 1700's was "childhood's greatest pleasure in the Pennsylvania Dutch country, next to the visit of the Christ-Kindel on Christmas Eve." Anticipation ran high as the children prepared a nest for the "Oschter Haws," as they called the Easter rabbit. They knew that if they had been good, he would come on Easter Eve and lay a whole nest full of colored eggs. Nests were built indoors in some secluded corner, in a sheltered place in the garden, or even in the barn. The Easter rabbit was a shy creature, hence the reason for a secluded spot. The boys used their caps and the girls their bonnets, or if father's old hat could be borrowed it might serve as the nest. Sometimes nests were made with fancy paper. The notions about elaborate baskets came much later when the tradition spread over the entire country.

For the strict religious sects, it was not truthful to tell the story of the Easter rabbit as the giver of eggs, so these families placed the gaily decorated gifts at the children's plates at the table or on the broad windowsills of the farmhouses.

Although this pleasant way of observing Easter was dear to the hearts of the German settlers wherever they made their homes in Pennsylvania, Virginia, the Carolinas, Tennessee, New York State, or Canada, it took more than a century before their English, Quaker, and Scotch-Irish neighbors adopted the custom. Children have a way of communicating ideas and enthusiasms which often make a deeper imprint than the sternest admonition from the pulpit. In the years following the Civil War, the Easter rabbit had become sufficiently popular to merit more than casual comment in the press each year as Easter approached. The various ways in which plain white or brown eggs could be decorated and the colorful designs which made them look like alluring jewels reflected the enduring quality of folk art, so integral a part of Pennsylvania Dutch culture. These sturdy people, whose love of the soil kept them close to the heritage of their homeland, had a way of expressing their faith, their folklore, and their love of life in simple art forms which captured the imagination of their neighbors.

A special kind of Easter cake made in the shape of a rabbit, using a raisin for an eye and a colored egg protruding beneath the rabbit's tail, was a popular practice in parts of the Dutch country. Local bakers made them in quantity, using the same dough they prepared for bread, and sometimes these cakes were home-made.

9
Winter Demons and Mardi Gras

Winter, the season of the year when vegetation is dormant, is a time of cold, often stormy weather, and short days. Darkness comes early and the resulting atmosphere is one of gloom. Before the development of modern lighting—when candles, pitch pine, and the fire on the hearth provided the only illumination—the atmosphere created by darkness was even more unpleasant. The peasants of Europe believed that the demons of winter were everywhere, lurking in the shadows of house and barn, in the fields and woods, and especially in dark places. In the Middle Ages, signs and symbols of these demons were to be found in the cold atmosphere, the leafless trees, the barren ground, and the brown grass. Only the death of Winter could dispel all this darkness.

The festival of Christmas, preceded by Advent and carrying through until Twelfth Night, provided a long period of joyous celebration to bring light into the dark days. Thus, the mummers appeared at the time of the winter solstice, dressed in strange costumes, with weird masques, dashing about shouting and making strange sounds. We still have them in some cities in parades at various seasons of the year. However uproarious and carefree these appear now, when their chief function is amusement, the spirit they represent is an ancient one—to scare away or drive out the demons of winter—the makers of darkness. Beginning with the revels of Twelfth Night and ending on Shrove Tuesday, celebrations and demonstrations of various kinds are linked with this fight against winter.

These rites took on a variety of forms. Fire was a strong and potent force. Wheels and hoops were rolled from high places, through fields and meadows, and torches were carried to drive out demon Winter. Sometimes, barrels of pitch were ignited and rolled downhill. Thus, the first Sunday of Lent is called Fire Sunday in southern Germany, and in France it is known as the Feast of the

Torches. Actually, the ancient peasant custom of making bonfires and dancing around them or leaping through them is much older than Christianity. Burning effigies is another closely associated practice.

Spring, midsummer, Halloween, and Christmas were the usual times for such pyrotechnics. At Easter, the fires were lighted on the first Sunday of Lent, presumably to burn the demon Winter, or banish the evil sower or, in some similar fashion, to assure fertility of the soil. Sometimes a fir or a beech tree was used as the center of activity for the fire. Brush was piled around it. Effigies such as a straw man, a witch, or an old wife attached to the tree were symbolic of destroying winter. The customs varied, in their procedures, costuming, and local associations, according to country, but the basic principle was the same.

On Easter Saturday, the symbolism relates to the new fire with which the Paschal candle is lighted in the churches and the good omen of such fire when brought to the hearth.

In Czechoslovakia, on a March day, the village folk make a dummy of old woman Winter, using a sack stuffed with straw. The children go from door to door carrying little trees hung with colored bows, singing as they go:

> "St. George, the Saint of spring,
> Will soon be here to unlock the earth with his keys.
> Our trees will soon grow,
> Like the ones we are holding."

Then they parade to the river, swinging old woman Winter from side to side, the townspeople following. As old woman Winter is thrown into the river and floats away, the people shout:

> "Death is floating down the river,
> And spring will soon be here."

In Zurich, Switzerland, the symbol of winter is a man called Bogg. On April 20th, they make a big wooden image of him, stuffing it with firecrackers and white cotton wool so that he will burn well. A parade with floats showing spring and her maidens ends with Bogg being carried to his doom. When the bells ring at six o'clock, the symbol of winter goes up in smoke.

Whatever the motivating force, the carnival spirit has its roots deep in the heart of man. The very word "carnival," which means literally "farewell to flesh," gives us the key to its significance. It is the time for the feasting, revelry, and gaiety that precede the long solemn Lenten fast, during which time, in bygone centuries, rigid rules of conduct prevailed. This celebration had its practical side also. Meat and its by-products were on the forbidden list for Lent, so these had to be used up before the season began. Hence, the Tuesday before Ash Wednesday became known as Fat Tuesday, or Mardi Gras. Butter Week and Fat Days were other names for this period in the calendar.

Among the people of the Latin countries particularly, the spirit of Mardi Gras is readily apparent. They show it in their infectious laughter and gaiety. In Paris, France, on the Tuesday before Lent, a huge ox is carried through the streets in a long procession consisting of the butchers of Paris. The fat ox is followed by the King of Butchers, who, strangely enough, is a small boy. The car in which the boy rides is filled with flowers, and sweets are thrown into the passing car by the crowds of spectators as tokens of greeting.

In Panama, King "Momo" rules with a wild, gay court each year during the four days preceding Ash Wednesday in celebration of the traditional carnival. This is the season when the people wear their colorful native costumes to dance the *Tamborito* and other traditional folk dances, and to sing *Guarore* and *Mi Negro*. This spectacle dates back to 1673, when the present city of Panama was founded. At first, Carnival was a mock ceremony commemorating the sacking of Old Panama by the pirates. Bands of young men dressed as pirates "attacked" the city, scaled the walls, and after fighting "battles" with other bands of "defenders," proceeded to "sack" the city. They carried off all the beautiful young girls to dances and parties, and kidnaped the wealthier citizens, who had to ransom themselves by buying rounds of drinks for the "pirates." Carnival as observed today was organized officially in 1910.

Today, everyone in Panama City dresses in *Pollero* and *Montuno* during the four days of Carnival. Bands of revelers roam the streets or drive around in cars, tossing confetti at bystanders. Each night, dances are held in the various clubs and restaurants, and in *toldos,* which are stands especially erected on street corners for the occasion. There are colorful parades, and a queen is chosen by popular vote from among the city's most beautiful debutantes.

The name Mardi Gras applies literally to one day only, the Tuesday before Ash Wednesday, but in New Orleans, the term Mardi Gras is used to refer to a six-day period which begins with the parade of Comus on the preceding Thursday evening and ends with the parade and ball in tribute to Comus on Shrove Tuesday, Mardi Gras night. Although Mardi Gras evolved from the original Carnival, Mardi Gras and Carnival are not synonymous in New Orleans. Each year Carnival is launched there on Twelfth Night with an elaborate ball. This marks the beginning of a long season of feasts, plays, masquerades, dances, and elaborate entertainment. In the early days, street travesties were popular. The exact day of the first Carnival observance has never been definitely established. Tradition has it that Jean Baptiste de Bienville, the founder of New Orleans, launched a celebration in 1718.

Local chroniclers claim that Mardi Gras began in 1827, the result of a revel by a group of young Creoles recently returned from private schools in Paris. Infected with the gay spirit of Paris, they donned weird costumes and danced merrily through the streets of the Old French Quarter. Prior to that time, the Carnival season was observed with fancy dress balls and masquerades held in private homes or auditoriums to which invitations were issued on the basis of social standing. The history of Mardi Gras for the past hundred years makes

 exciting reading and few have told it better than Hartnett Kane in his *Queen New Orleans, City by the River,* and other books from his pen.

In 1857, an organization known as the Mistick Krewe of Comus was formed to manage the event. Fifteen years later, Rex, the acknowledged ruler of Mardi Gras, began his reign. In the years that have followed, other groups or societies have been organized. Each year Mardi Gras grows bigger and bigger, with more and more excitement, until it would seem that local residents know only two seasons of the year—Carnival and after the Carnival. As Mr. Kane has written, "He who tastes of Mississippi water, he'll be back. . . . He who tastes of Mardi Gras, he will also return. It's the maddest, fastest, giddiest, most absurd, most magnificent thing in New Orleans."

In Biloxi, Mississippi, there is a Mardi Gras celebration that is claimed to be older than that held in New Orleans, since the city was founded in 1699. Mobile, Alabama, began its observance in 1830. All three cities vie with one another for publicity and all that goes with it to make visitors welcome in Carnival time.

10
Forty Days and Easter

Innumerable legends and scores of traditions and folk beliefs are associated with the Lenten season and Eastertide. Because many of these observances have special significance for those who profess them, they are described in an attempt to record typical kinds of services, without including all the details which make them distinctive. It is not pertinent to this account to enumerate all of them or to explain their symbolism. Then too, there still remain many quaint old customs, long since neglected, that have not been recorded. These are carried in the memories of folk in remote villages, having been passed down from generation to generation in the great oral tradition so prevalent in many parts of the Old World. The lore included in this chapter is, in most instances, familiar in many parts of Europe, but many of the customs are little known in the United States.

Since Francis X. Weiser, in *The Easter Book* and *The Handbook of Christian Feasts and Customs,* has presented a vivid picture of the liturgy of this holy season, no attempt has been made to present here this information in its entirety. In Chapter 7, "Foods of the Easter Season," many days of lesser importance are discussed in relation to the foods served and the traditions associated with them.

ASH WEDNESDAY

"Remember, man, that thou art dust, and to dust thou shalt return," is the central theme of the solemn services in Roman Catholic churches on Ash Wednesday. These words are repeated as the priest makes the sign of the Cross on the forehead of each member of the congregation who approaches the altar for the distribution of ashes. The ashes are made from burned palm leaves saved from the previous Palm Sunday. This symbol of penance and sorrow for one's

sins marks the beginning of the day on which Christ fasted in the wilderness. For nearly a thousand years, the first day of Lent has been known as Ash Wednesday. Prior to that time it was called the "Beginning of the Fast."

In the twentieth century, the practices of fasting during Lent are much less severe than they were in the early days of the Christian era. Abstaining meant giving up the use of all flesh meat and all its by-products such as milk, cheese, butter, and eggs. Only those in delicate health were released from this rigid practice. In many countries, Roman Catholics still abide by this stringent fast for the entire forty days of Lent, even on Sundays, which are not included in the regulations. Originally, only one meal a day was allowed, usually in the evening, with only water allowed at intervals during the day.

The opening of the Lenten season is observed with special services in most of the Protestant churches in the United States and elsewhere around the world. While no obligation of fast and abstinence is imposed by regulation among the various denominations, it has long been customary for Protestants to deny themselves some favorite food, pastime, or luxury during Lent. However, any form of self-denial practiced or encouraged by a particular denomination is based on the convictions of the individual and is not a required part of the creed professed. In the *Book of Common Prayer* used in the Episcopal Church, days of fast and abstinence are designated.

The solemn tone of preparation for Easter has been little changed in the Roman Catholic, the Greek Orthodox, and the Episcopal churches through the centuries. The pleasures of the flesh are put aside for contemplation of the things of the spirit. For centuries, this day was also one of public penance for those whose misdeeds were known, and pardon was sought not only through the confessional, but by carrying out prescribed acts of humility in public. Then on Holy Thursday, the penitents appeared in church to receive absolution.

In Spain, the presentation of a miracle play was an old tradition of this solemn day. The characters included Joseph with his lily-crowned staff, Mary Magdalene wearing black curls which hung down to her knees, Pilate as a kindly old gentleman, the Wandering Jew and, at the end, the Mother of Sorrows, sitting alone in her sorrow.

"Burying the sardine" on Ash Wednesday is an old custom which is still observed at the close of Mardi Gras in New Orleans. Originally, it consisted of burying a strip of meat as thin as a sardine, as a reminder of the rigid fast imposed in Lent. Another curious tradition of Spain was the making of a weird effigy of a woman with seven legs. The legs represented the seven weeks of Lent, and the strange figure, made of cardboard, was known as the queen of Lent. She was paraded about and each week one of her legs was removed, until in Passion Week she was burned in a pyre.

PALM SUNDAY

"Blessed is he that cometh in the name of the Lord! Hosanna in the highest," was the cry of joy on the lips of the throng that greeted Jesus on his triumphant entry into Jerusalem on that first day of Passover Week. This Prophet who had achieved a reputation for His message of hope and His acts of healing was hailed by many who believed he was the Messiah, and that he would free them from Roman domination. Breaking branches of the date palm and the olive, they strewed them on the streets and waved them about as a sign of welcome.

Each year, in the majority of Christian churches throughout the world, the significance of Palm Sunday is intoned with special music and inspired sermons to commemorate the day. Palms are distributed at the close of the services, or they are used to decorate altars, chancels, and communion tables. In recent years, the use of palm has become widespread among many Christian denominations, although some groups distribute it only at Sunday School rather than at the regular Palm Sunday services. In like manner, many of the ancient liturgical customs and ceremonial practices of the early Church are being adapted, in one way or another, to give greater symbolic meaning to traditional forms of Protestant service, as well as to new expressions of worship. This trend has had marked significance, particularly with regard to the observance of the Lenten season. In practically every instance where there has been a revival of interest in liturgical forms, it has been introduced either by an individual clergyman or a lay member of a congregation and is not a specific part of a creed.

Visitors to Rome during Easter Week are always eager to attend the ceremonies at St. Peter's Basilica, where the Pope is borne aloft in an elaborate procession for the blessing of the palms. Great bunches of palm leaves, sometimes ornately arranged and festooned, are carried by attendants. In countries where palm is not available, sprays of such greens as the willow, the boxwood, the yew, the olive, and other greens are used on this day—"Sunday of the Palm Carrying," as it is referred to in Greece. Small crosses made of palm leaves are often attached to the sprays of the substitute plants. Branch Sunday, Willow-twig Sunday, and Hosanna Sunday are other names for this day of ceremony.

Francis X. Weiser, in *The Easter Book,* describing the liturgy of the day, relates that it was customary in Catholic churches "to bless not only branches, but various flowers of the season (the flowers are still mentioned in the antiphons after the prayer of blessing)." Thus we have the origin of the name Flowering, or Blossom Sunday. In some countries, visits are made to the churchyards where the graves are tidied up and decorated with flowers.

The day was known as Fig Sunday because fig pudding was served, and bunches of figs were given to the children as reminders of the Parable of the Barren Fig. Spanish Sunday is another name for the day in English folklore, because children used to make a drink from pieces of Spanish liquorice and water from a holy wishing well. Chare or Shere Sunday is also of English origin, referring to the ceremony of clearing the altars for Easter. The modern habit of spring house cleaning, often done prior to Easter, is undoubtedly an offshoot of this practice.

Many fascinating customs referring to farm practices are associated with Palm Sunday. In Sicily, dust from the floor of the church was swept up to be

scattered on the fields. The direction in which the wind blew for most of the day would determine its direction for the coming summer, according to an old English record. A clear day on Palm Sunday was indicative of good weather, abundant grain and plenty of fruit. Branches of olive and fir trees were blessed in Dalmatian churches and carried home to be placed over the entrances or scattered in the fields. Pussy willows blessed in church were waved above the grain fields in Russia to insure a good crop. At Rapallo, Italy, the eggs of the silkworm were taken to church to be blessed.

Carol singing was a feature in Macedonian villages where the girls carried handsomely embroidered handkerchiefs and sang carols to please young and old. A curious custom in Mexico was the carrying of elaborately decorated crosses to church on Palm Sunday. These were decorated with flowers, fruits, and cakes donated by friends, and the couple who succeeded in gathering the greatest number of gifts for the cross and the pole were obviously rated high in the popularity of the community.

MAUNDY THURSDAY

Holy Thursday, also known as Maundy Thursday, marks the feast of the Last Supper, the washing of the feet of His disciples by Christ, and the message of brotherly love which He gave to His disciples. "A new commandment I give unto you, that ye love one another." This was a new mandate, which in the French is spelled *maunde,* one explanation for the name Maundy Thursday. A similar Anglo-Saxon term referred to a basket, or maund, from which bread was distributed to the poor by the titled women of the great houses of Europe. Hence the practice of Queen Elizabeth II of distributing alms on this day, which had been done by the Royal Almoner prior to the time of George V. In Queen Victoria's time, Maundy money was coined especially for the day.

Each year, the Pope washes the feet of thirteen men in St. Peter's. Twelve represent the apostles, and the thirteenth symbolizes the angel who came to the table, according to tradition, when Gregory the Great was officiating at the Last Supper ceremony in the sixth century. In monasteries, the members of the order performed this act for as many men as they were years old. There is a quaint account of Queen Elizabeth, of sixteenth-century fame, who performed the act in a room decorated with willow branches which were arranged to give the effect of palms. She was attended each year by ladies-in-waiting who numbered as many as the birthdays she had observed. The ceremony of washing the feet of the poor was performed three times, first by the yeoman of the guard, then by the Royal Almoner, and finally by the Queen herself. Fresh herbs were floated in the bowl of warm water that was used. Then gifts of food were given to those who had received the Queen's attention. This practice has long since been replaced by the giving of Maundy money. The ceremony, usually held at Westminster Abbey, is performed with great dignity.

Sometimes, this day is also referred to as Green Thursday, or the Day of the

Green Ones, in reference to the old custom of re-admitting penitents to the church. (In the early days of the Roman Church, those who had committed serious sins appeared at church on Ash Wednesday to beg forgiveness and receive penance which they carried out during the Lenten fast.) The penitents wore sprigs of green herbs to express their joy and were referred to as the "green ones." Green vestments were worn by the priests for the same reason. According to German tradition, the word "green" is a corruption of a term of somewhat similar sound which means "to mourn." The eating of green vegetables is a customary part of the meals served on this day in many parts of Europe and, to some extent, in the United States.

The folk-name, "Kiss Thursday," recalled the Kiss of Judas. The old name Shier or Sher Thursday is derived from the practice of men shearing their beards for grief at the betrayal of the Saviour.

The re-enactment of the Last Supper, which takes place in Rome, is also dramatized in Roman Catholic churches in Central and South America. Silencing of the steeple bells as well as those used at Mass, and the termination of music in church, are old practices of this Feast Day. Children were told that the bells had gone to Rome to visit the tombs of the martyrs and to be blessed by the Pope. There the bells remain until Easter Saturday, according to French tradition. Upon returning, they bring the Easter eggs to be given to all good children. Another occasion for singing by the young people occurs in rural Germany and Austria on this day. In lieu of bells, wooden clappers are used to sound out the time of day. Boys go about carrying wooden clappers, and like town criers, call out the time of day, as they continuously sing of Eastertide.

In recent years, the "Meal in the Upper Room" has become a special Holy Week service in some Protestant churches. Traditional Passover food, similar to that eaten in the Holy Land in the time of the Saviour, is served. In the Hebrew tradition, food shared together has always been in itself a pledge of friendship and loyalty. The meal includes lamb, cheese, spinach, rice, olives, matzoths (unleavened bread), grapes, figs, walnuts, and grape juice. The service is carried out in silence, interspersed with readings from the Gospel and the Psalms.

A large seven-branch candelabra, typical of the kind used at Passover, is lighted when all have gathered at the table, and the room is illuminated entirely by candlelight. Selections from Psalm 113 from the Hebrew *Hallel* are read as the candles are lighted, followed by the Passover Thanksgiving Prayer, taken from the same source, Psalm 118.

GOOD FRIDAY

Purple drapery in some form, used to conceal the figures of the saints in Roman Catholic churches where altars have been stripped of all ceremonial objects, sounds the keynote of sadness and mourning that marks Good Friday as a day of fasting and prayer. From the beginning, this solemn day of Lent

has been given personal significance, as the anguish and the suffering of the crucified Christ were conveyed to the members of the congregation through prayers and preaching. Such names as Holy Friday, Friday of Mourning, Long Friday, God's Friday, and Great Friday indicate its significance in various countries.

A service of hymns and prayers known as the "Three Hours" has become a custom in churches of various Christian denominations in the United States and several European countries in recent years. A series of short sermons on the "Seven Last Words," interspersed with hymns and prayers, begins at noon and ends at three o'clock. In the United States in recent years, many commercial enterprises close during this time to give people an opportunity to attend services. As in some countries of Europe, Good Friday has become a legal holiday in the United States in eleven states.

Devotion to the solemnity of Good Friday expresses itself in a variety of ways among the peoples of Europe. In both England and France, a dramatic ceremony built around a replica of the Holy Sepulcher is an expression of piety which made the crucifixion story very real. It was the custom in the early days to form a procession within the church after the Passion had been sung, and place a cross or the Blessed Sacrament, or both, in shrines or tabernacles, shaped like a tomb, at a side altar. Members of the congregation venerated this tabernacle throughout the day and again on Holy Saturday. Lighted candles, palms, and flowers were used for decoration. In some countries, an honor guard garbed in the uniform of the country, or wearing the insignia of a religious organization, kept the vigil in atonement for the guard of Roman soldiers on the first Good Friday.

In the Old World, little or no work is done on this day. Household chores such as weaving and laundering are taboo. It has long been a belief that clothes washed on this day will be marked or spotted. Yet, a loaf of bread baked on Good Friday will never become moldy. It is considered a good day to move bees, to plant parsley, beans and peas, and to graft fruited trees. Rain that falls is bottled, as it is believed to be a cure for eye troubles. In the days of blacksmiths, no self-respecting craftsman would drive a nail, because of the use to which hammer and nails were put on Good Friday. Iron, so tradition goes, should not be driven into the ground for the same reason.

The hallowing of rings is an old tradition of English kings dating back to the days of Edward the Confessor in the eleventh century. Certain rings worn to prevent falling sickness were taken to church by the king to be blessed during the ceremony of the Adoration of the Cross.

The memory of Judas was kept alive at the church at St. Croce in Florence, Italy. On Good Friday morning, it was the custom for the boys to obtain bunches of willow tied with colored ribbons which they took to church. At a point in the service, they beat the pews with the willow rods and gave vent to their feelings as they thrashed Judas. In England, boys hunted squirrels because

of the old fable that Judas was transformed into a creature of this group of rodents.

The English custom of playing marbles on Good Friday is an ancient one and probably had its origin in Holland or Belgium. Boys young and old played the game all day on their way to church and on the way home. This fascinating game has all but disappeared in the twentieth century. Playing marbles on Good Friday may have been a vestige of the dice-throwing of the Roman soldiers at the foot of the cross.

Some tribes of gypsies would not use water on this day because Pilate washed his hands at Christ's trial. Pottery broken on Good Friday was not a total loss, for every piece of it would bruise Judas.

In England, skipping rope, sailing boats, and catching shellfish were engaged in by families. This was the day for hot cross buns, which were not only good to eat, but served as a charm against bad luck if hung in the house and kept till the following year. They might get black and dusty, but it was believed that they would not get moldy. As a keepsake, two people would break a bun within the church, each party keeping half to retain a friendly bond.

Ethel L. Urlin, a noted English folklorist who wrote at the turn of the century, described a Good Friday procession in Spain which had all the impressive beauty of a passion play. The images used in the procession were the work of a medieval wood sculptor, and each group of figures on parade was handled by a trade guild. "The tailors bear the gigantic group of the Last Supper, the gardeners, that of the Agony in the Garden, the bakers, the Kiss of Judas; the shoemakers the group of St. John. . . . All the bearers are dressed in violet and carry candles and musical instruments. A standard bearer comes first, accompanied by a group of boys whose duty it is to proclaim to the crowd—'This is done in remembrance of the Passion of Our Lord Jesus Christ'—announced with bells and trumpets." The ancient wood carver, whose work was of extraordinary beauty, had long since become a legendary figure. It was claimed by those who viewed the parade that he had chiseled out the Agony in the Garden from a drawing furnished him by an angel which he had received into his home as a poor man seeking a night's lodging.

EASTER DAY

Easter Saturday or Easter Eve is often referred to as a day of preparation for the "Lord's Day of Joy." The ceremonies of the day, which include the blessing of the water, the Paschal candle, and new fire, are traditional among Catholics. When blessing the water for baptism took place, it was the custom in many parts of Europe to bless the rivers, the wells, and the brooks also. In both Catholic and Episcopal churches, new fire used to be kindled at midnight by striking a flint against steel. People gathered in a darkened church to remind them of Christ in the tomb as they witnessed the making of light. Once the

flint was struck against steel and flame was made, the Paschal candle was lighted, and then followed the lighting of other candles in the church.

In that famed cathedral, the Duomo at Florence, Italy, there was an old custom called the "Ceremony of the Cart." A dove, carrying a lighted fragment from the high altar, flew along a wire out the western door. It was supposed to ignite a cart, signifying the fruits of the earth. If successful, a prosperous harvest was assured for the ensuing year.

The importance of wearing new clothes at Easter is older than the dictates of fashion or high-powered advertising. In the early days of Christianity, it was at Easter that baptism was administered to converts, and after the ceremony they put on white garments as a sign of joy. However small or insignificant the bit of new wearing apparel may be, it must be something new that is worn on Easter Day—even a pair of shoelaces, a bit of ribbon, or a fresh feather. Woe to him who did not heed this custom, for the crows (or the pigeons or some other bird) would single out the culprit and put their own mark on him! For centuries, even in pagan times, it was the custom to put on new clothes for the spring festivals. A pair of gloves sent to a girl on Easter Eve meant that her suitor had serious intentions and, if the recipient wore these, marriage was more or less assured.

In Bavaria, the burning of the Easter Man takes place on Holy Saturday, when a straw figure, bound to a tall cross, is lighted with new fire brought from the church. On Easter Monday the ashes are scattered on the fields.

Fires lighted on the hills or in cemeteries on this night attract young folks who dance around the fires and sometimes leap over them. Flaming torches are often carried through the fields to bring good fortune for the crops.

The delight of children in dressing up in costumes to sing carols, beg for Easter eggs, and to carry messages finds expression in a variety of customs in all the countries of Europe. An unusually quaint practice, which may be the forerunner of Easter greetings as we use them today, had its origin in Sweden. An Easter letter with a picture of a witch on a broomstick and a message of good will was slipped under the door, followed by firecrackers that were lighted in the road. This performance is accounted for by the belief that the witches of Sweden met at Easter to hold a session with the devil. In olden times, fires were lighted and gunpowder was shot off to drive these flying creatures away.

The Easter Eve vigil was observed in the early days of Christianity in the midst of great illumination. In some countries kings set up great pillars of wax to make their cities as bright as day. Candles, lamps, and torches were used by private citizens in front of their homes. In the churches, the great Paschal candle, and quantities of smaller tapers, symbols of Christ as the maker of light, provided the gleam and glory that must have made a profound impression on the faithful as they waited through the night of watching for the dawn.

An account of a ceremony in the Cathedral of Sofia in Bulgaria, written fifty years ago, told of a multitude of several thousand who waited outside the Cathedral, with only one light flickering in a small window. Then a great procession of priests in their brocaded vestments accompanied by monks and acolytes and uniformed soldiers, followed by the leaders of the community, marched up to the great west door. The Bishop struck the door with his foot as the choir poured forth: "Lift up your heads, O ye gates, and be ye lift up, ye everlasting doors, that the King of Glory may come in!" The response from the lighted window came—"Who is the King of Glory?" Following the refrain from the choir and the response from above, the doors were flung open and the Cathedral became a blaze of light. After the service, the Prince of Bulgaria greeted his guests, including ambassadors from other countries. Then baskets of colored eggs marked in gold with the royal monogram were brought in and distributed.

The Lord's Supper, in life-size wax figures, an interpretation of Leonardo DaVinci's famous painting, *The Last Supper*, on permanent display at 6209 Sunset Drive, Fort Worth, Texas.

11
The Holy Grail

There are veritable libraries of legend, romance, and allegory concerning the Holy Grail, the cup or chalice used by Christ at the Last Supper. However, no book about Easter would be complete without a brief account of this mystic vessel.

The legend that accounts for the existence of the chalice is actually a series of ancient tales richly colored with symbolism and mysticism. Even in its simplest form, it is a story best presented as a parent would tell it to his children.

Before the time of Adam and Eve, God once left His throne to visit His new creation, Earth, and to appraise it. In God's absence, Lucifer, one of the highest of the angels, seized this opportunity to demand that the angels pay homage to him. To indicate that they were subservient to him, Lucifer demanded that they create for him a crown of wondrous beauty. This wish was granted, but soon came the downfall. Michael, gathering the faithful angels of God, quickly quelled the rebels, and, as Lucifer and his crew hurtled from heaven, one of the precious stones detached itself from the crown and dropped to earth, unnoticed.

Next, Lucifer was found to be scheming to seduce Adam and Eve, then newly created by God. Learning of the plan, God placed a guard of angels around Adam and Eve to protect them. Unfortunately, the youngest angel of the guard, Israfil, consumed with curiosity, left his post to gaze at the sleeping Eve. Then it was that Satan entered the Garden of Eden unnoticed and induced Eve to eat the forbidden fruit. Not only were Adam and Eve punished by God

after this catastrophe, but also the angel, Israfil, who was condemned to be the angel of death and destruction, and as such, was shunned by all. Israfil could not have endured all of this had not the Son of God suddenly appeared to him in a dream, telling him that God would give the Redeemer the power of restoring life to the dead birds and flowers, and that He would also give everlasting life and happiness to all those whom Israfil had slain. Thus, the sad-faced angel went forth to do God's will and visited Abel, Adam and Eve, whom he greatly admired, and then dogged the footsteps of all the human race.

The precious stone which had fallen from Lucifer's crown was eventually found and fashioned into a priceless cup. After many centuries, this vessel came into the hands of Joseph of Arimathea, a man of wealth and prestige, in whose house Christ kept the feast of the Passover with His disciples. The Crucifixion followed the next day and Joseph, taking this cup, stood beneath the Cross to receive a few drops of the blood of Christ. Because of this incident, the vessel was called Sangraal, or Holy Grail, for the divine blood had not only sanctified it but had also given it miraculous powers which soon became known.

Joseph asked for the body of Christ so that he might bury it in a new tomb which he had built. The Jewish people learned this and, fearful that Caesar might wish to claim the body which they could not produce, resolved to kill Joseph of Arimathea. They took him by night, and placed him in a sealed prison cell where it was believed that he would die. However, he was marvelously fed and sustained by the Holy Grail's beams of life-giving light. The Roman Emperor Vespasian finally learned the truth about Joseph and had him freed from the prison. That he came out alive, although he had been walled in, was a surprise to all.

This was not his last trial with the Jews; fearing them, Joseph sailed away to Marseilles in France, carrying the precious Holy Grail with him. He was accompanied by his sister, his brother-in-law, and a number of the followers of Christ. Besides supplying them with the food and drink which they liked best, the Holy Grail, whose beneficent powers were renewed every Good Friday (because a dove brought from heaven a consecrated wafer that was deposited in the cup), cured them when they were ill, and also served as an oracle! When Joseph and his friends did not know what to do on a given occasion, they prayed and then consulted the edge of the Holy Grail, where they could read commands which appeared in letters of flame as replies.

Thus they were happy in France until one of them committed a secret sin. Plague and famine broke out, and Joseph was given orders by the Holy Grail to build a Round Table and to make a supper to which all were invited. Then, the culprit of the crime would be designated so that when Moses was swallowed up by the earth, his vacated chair would be called "Siege Perilous." Furthermore, it would be fatal for all who sat in it, that is, all except one of Joseph of Arimathea's descendants, a knight of stainless reputation.

According to popular tradition, a short time later, Joseph carried the Holy

Grail to Glastonbury, in England. (Scholars of the Glastonbury legend maintain that Joseph brought to England a pair of cruets containing a relic of the Saviour's blood, and not the mystic vessel.) He went to the fabled land of Avalon, "where falls no hail, or rain, or any snow." By now, Joseph of Arimathea was tired of wandering, so he thrust his staff deep into the ground, where it miraculously took root and bloomed at Christmas time as the famous Glastonbury thorn.

Joseph and his followers established the first monastery at Glastonbury and they kept guard over the Holy Grail. Years passed and the sacred cup remained visible to the good. But sin occurred and the Holy Grail was carried away by the angels. From time to time some especially favored mortal was permitted to view the Holy Grail, which plays such an important role in the legends of King Arthur, of the operas, "Parsifal" and "Lohengrin."

In the nineteenth century, Alfred Lord Tennyson gave the story of the Holy Grail to his host of readers in the "Idylls of the King." He drew on sources from the Middle Ages, since the great collection of legends that comprise this fabulous story had its roots in early Welsh, English, Celtic, and French sources.

The Once and Future King, by T. B. White, was made into a musical comedy entitled *Camelot,* by Allan J. Lerner and Frederick Loewe in 1960 and played to throngs in the theaters. A powerfully drawn novel by Thomas B. Costain entitled *The Silver Chalice* gives present-day readers another concept of the Holy Grail. Mr. Costain writes of Basil of Antioch, a young and skilled artisan who created a decorative chasing for the precious chalice. One may well conjecture that the author must have stood often before the Chalice of Antioch displayed in The Cloister Collection in the New York Metropolitan Museum of Art. This fifth-century silver vessel used in the sacrament of the Lord's Supper was discovered near Antioch by a group of Arabs who were digging a well. Engraved on the chalice is a symbolic eagle with outspread wings, perched upon a basket of Eucharistic bread. Christ's throne rises above the bird as though supported by its wings. While He stretches out his arm in blessing, a dove flies above. The grapevine encircling the chalice represents the Church. Besides the eagle and the dove, eight other birds are depicted, together with the apostles and small, decorative creatures—truly an awe-inspiring work of art wrought with the utmost skill.

H. Armstrong Roberts

12
A Seal with a Symbol

The Easter traditions we cherish in America have come to us from the Old World. The Easter bunny, the Sunrise Service, described in the following chapter, the Easter lily and the wealth of folk customs that have been blended with our way of life are adaptations often colored with a distinct American flair. They are ours by inheritance, to cherish and to keep alive. However, the great humanitarian movement that launched the annual Easter Seal drive for aid to crippled children is truly American. Yet, the idea of using seals to raise money for charitable purposes came from Elmer Holboll, a Danish postal clerk, in 1903. He it was who originated the Christmas seals for the control of tuberculosis.

On Memorial Day, 1907, in Elyria, Ohio, a streetcar accident occurred, involving a group of young people returning from a holiday excursion. Many died of injuries that could not be properly treated in the town hospital. Others were maimed for life. The effects of this tragic accident might have been confined to one remote community, but the event was destined to have world-wide significance. Fourteen years later, the National Society for Crippled Children and Adults was founded. This organization of volunteers is dedicated to a program of enlightening the public on what can be done for the crippled, and of mobilizing public and private resources to develop needed services.

One of the boys who died in the tragic accident in Ohio was eighteen-year-old Homer Allen. The boy's father, Edgar F. Allen, keenly aware of the inadequacy of local hospital facilities, spearheaded a drive for a new general hospital. A crippled boy who was brought to the hospital made Mr. Allen aware of a new and different need—that of crippled children for special medical care and treat-

ment. He saw what proper care had achieved in restoring the boy from a hopeless condition to one of optimism and expectation for a normal life. Then, he began to visualize what it would mean to countless others to have similar care. Through his contact with the boy, who dubbed him affectionately "Daddy," Edgar Allen was led into the activity which was to be a life-long career of service.

Once his interest was aroused, the first logical steps for "Daddy" Allen were to conduct a survey to find out how many crippled children there were in his home county and to organize community support to build the Gates Memorial Hospital for Crippled Children. He then embarked on an even more ambitious program of arranging for crippled children elsewhere in Ohio to be brought to the hospital, where care and treatment were provided without cost. To accomplish this great humanitarian task, he enlisted the interest and support of Rotarians. In turn, it was the Rotarians who spearheaded the founding in Ohio in 1919 of the first state crippled children's society, an organization of volunteers dedicated to a program which provided privately supported services, while it sought extension and increased support for public services for the crippled.

The program of the Ohio society flourished. By 1921, "Daddy" Allen saw sufficient evidence of similar interest on the part of Rotarians in Michigan, New York, and Illinois to convince him that the time had come for national action. He sought official endorsement of expansion of the "Ohio Plan" through Rotary International. Although Paul P. Harris, founder of Rotary, was particularly receptive to the idea and did much to promote it, formal action did not come about. However, the interest shown by the Rotarians in the problem greatly aided the spread of the crippled children's movement throughout the nation.

Meanwhile, in 1921 a dedicated group of volunteers, headed by "Daddy" Allen, launched the National Society for Crippled Children, with headquarters in Elyria, Ohio. The first President was "Daddy" Allen, who served until 1937.

In the early years, he stimulated much of the interest among Rotarians singlehandedly. Later, he was aided by a small staff. Once the National Society was launched, the movement spread quickly. Michigan and New York societies were organized in 1922. Kentucky, Pennsylvania, Tennessee, West Virginia, and Illinois followed in 1923. By the end of 1929, there were twenty-three state societies for crippled children.

The Society was a pioneer in its field. It stood alone at that time as the only national voluntary agency speaking and acting on behalf of the crippled. Federal-state crippled children's programs were not enacted for almost a decade. The Federal Vocational Rehabilitation Act of 1920 provided for a very limited program and was not to be expanded for more than twenty years. State tax-supported programs were very few. Prior to the founding of the Society, there was no concerted attack on the problem of rehabilitating the crippled citizens of America, either by voluntary or public agencies.

The Crippled Child, a magazine, was established in 1923. A Bureau of Information and Library began operation in 1924. One of the greatest tasks of the National Society in the early years was to encourage and aid in the drafting of special state legislation to meet the medical, educational, and vocational needs of the crippled. In 1935, provisions were made in the Social Security Act, due largely to the efforts of the Society.

In 1922, the name of the Society was changed to International Society for Crippled Children in order to encourage the development of similar voluntary organizations in other countries. Eight years later it became advisable to separate the national and the international organizations.

It was in 1934 that the Easter Seal was adopted as a fund-raising device. The conventionalized Easter lily, adopted in 1952 as the symbol of the organization, is now widely known, and the societies for crippled children and adults are called informally, "The Easter Seal Societies."

In 1945, headquarters of the National Society were moved to Chicago. In succeeding years, the national organization was extended to include state and local member societies in all of the forty-eight states, the District of Columbia, and the then territories of Alaska and Hawaii, as well as Puerto Rico. A national staff of professional consultants in care and treatment, organization, public education, and fund raising was developed.

The Easter Seal Research Foundation was established in 1953, thus creating a means for implementing a third major objective of the Society, added to those of care and treatment and education that had been pursued since 1921. In 1958, the national headquarters built and occupied its own building in the West Side Medical Center in Chicago.

Services, which started literally with care for one crippled child, in 1957 reached more than 160,000 crippled children and adults. These direct services are provided by more than 1600 state and local affiliates which operate some 1400 rehabilitation and treatment centers, clinics, camps, sheltered workshops, home employment, physical, occupational and speech therapy programs, and other related services. The professional personnel staffing these programs, together with administrative personnel, have reached a total of more than 2000.

In 1933, Paul H. King, who followed Mr. Allen as president of the society, originated the idea of selling Easter seals. As he expressed it, "Thoughts of Easter and the crippled child harmonize wonderfully. Easter means Resurrection and New Life; and the rehabilitation of crippled children means . . . new life and activity, complete or partial, physically, mentally, and spiritually."

The first seal was designed by J. H. Donahey, the famous cartoonist of the Cleveland *Plain Dealer*. Copies of the 1934 seal have become exceedingly scarce, and prices quoted to collectors by dealers are on the increase. The next two seals were also based on appealing cartoons drawn by Mr. Donahey. After the 1935 Easter seal sale, nobody doubted any longer that the Easter seal for crippled children was here to stay. From twenty-two million in 1934, distribution of Easter seals has risen to more than a billion. Nearly three million dollars worth of seals are now sold annually, and the distribution is constantly on the upgrade.

Courtesy National Pa

Easter Morning 6:46 A.M. Mountain Standard Time in the Amphitheater, Mount Rushmore National Memorial.

13
The Glory of the Sun

Long ago, it was believed that Easter Day was best begun by rising early enough to see the sun dance as it rose in the sky. If the viewers were in the right spot and carried a piece of smoked glass to look through, they might see the symbol of the Risen Saviour—the image of the Lamb of God with the banner marked with a red cross. It was sometimes referred to as "the lamb playing." Instead of walking in the fields, there were those among the country folk in the British Isles who placed a pan of water in an east window that they might see the reflection of the sun as it danced. This old myth was the subject of considerable discussion in the seventeenth and eighteenth centuries, and even earlier. Some scorned it; others pondered the idea philosophically, and still other writers recorded it for what they believed it to be—mere superstition.

Yet, men have seen strange and wonderful sights in the sky at various hours of the day, century after century, down through the ages. Who can challenge the flights of imagination to which some men are subject or the visions which they claim? Surely, there are many forms of imagery that have meaning for those who experienced them.

In France, there is an old belief that the rays of sunlight penetrating the dawn clouds on Easter morning are angels dancing for joy at the Resurrection. It used to be said in Scotland that the sun whirled around like a mill wheel and gave three leaps. An old Irish custom was a dance of joy to greet the sun on this day. The women of the village baked a cake for a prize, and the men performed the dance. The best dancer was awarded the cake, and from this bit of jollity came the expression, "he takes the cake." Dancing to honor the sun after the vernal equinox is associated with the lore of many countries.

Among the many curious folk-beliefs relating to Easter morning is an ancient practice once observed on the Island of Malta. The men of the community made their way to the village church and transported a statue of Christ to a nearby promontory, running uphill as fast as they could while ceremoniously carrying aloft the revered figure. This rapid movement signified the Resurrection.

It was on an Easter morning, March 27, 1513, that Ponce de Leon first sighted the land which he named Florida, from the Spanish *Pasqua Florida*. The words originally meant Palm Sunday, but were later applied to the entire Easter week. Centuries later, on Easter Day, 1722, a Dutchman named Roggeveen expressed his feeling of joy and hope when he discovered an island in the Southeast Pacific which was named Easter Island. Often referred to as "the loneliest little island in the world," the natives called it "Eye which sees heaven," and "Frontier of Heaven."

The folklore and the traditions of every country in the world are, to a large extent, the accumulated customs and manners blended with signs and symbols that serve as reminders of religious practices and historic associations. In those countries that are rich in folk culture, one nationality is dominant; such a homogeneous atmosphere is conducive to the creation and development of a distinctive folklore. When national groups have colonized new areas of the world, they have, in most instances, perpetuated their beloved customs and traditions which live on, slightly changed and in new guise, but ever cherished as links with the past. Such is the Easter sunrise service, which has become popular all over America in recent years.

"Millions of Americans will greet Easter this year with sunrise services of worship: the first of these at the summit of Cadillac Mountain on Mt. Desert Island, Maine, where the sun first touches the United States, and then in hundreds of similar services as the dawn moves westward across the land.

"There will be sunrise services in nineteen of our National Parks, including Grand Canyon and Death Valley, and on our Navy ships at sea. At Aspen, Colorado, worshipers will travel by ski lift for services atop 11,300-foot Ajax Mountain. Perhaps 100,000 people will gather at midnight Easter Eve in the mountains near Lawton, Oklahoma, to witness a six-hour pageant depicting episodes from the life of Christ and concluding at dawn with the Resurrection story. Other thousands will assemble in the vast outdoor amphitheater at the Park of the Red Rocks at Denver, and a reverent multitude will fill the Hollywood Bowl." Thus, Joseph R. Siroo, of George Washington University, recently described the widespread scope of Easter sunrise services in various parts of the United States.

A group of Spaniards exploring North America, from Key West to Southern California, are believed to have held the first sunrise service on Easter Sunday in the year 1609. The Moravians who settled at Winston-Salem, North Carolina, in 1773, established a beautiful custom which continues to this day. With great dignity and true religious fervor, they gather in front of the old Home Moravian Church several hours before daybreak, to give the traditional salutations that open the service, *The Lord Is Risen!* Continuing with other hymns of joy that express their simple faith, they walk quietly in long lines as day breaks, to God's Acre, the Moravian cemetery. There they reaffirm their faith. Great throngs of visitors gather each year to witness this ceremony, which reflects the cherished beliefs of a sect that has preserved its folk customs in all their simplicity and beauty.

A similar service takes place in Bethlehem, Pennsylvania, where the Moravian Trombone Choir, organized in 1754, adds greatly to the annual Easter sunrise service. The choir moves through the center of the city playing chorales at the principal intersections of downtown streets between midnight and dawn, and then proceeds to the church, where part of the service is conducted. In accordance with old custom, the remainder of the observance is held in the churchyard. A second service is given later in the morning, and a third at night. An account of the beginning of this impressive ceremony, written by J. Max Hark for the Lancaster *Intelligencer,* April 24, 1886, gives us a word-picture couched in the elegant phrases of the Victorian era.

"Very early on Sunday morning, long before the first penciling of dawn gives outline to the darkness, there mingle strangely with the sleepers' dreams the sounds of far-off soft and sweetest melody. Wafted from a distance through the fresh and fragrant morning air, like angels' whispers from on high they seem, as gently falling on the semi-conscious ear. Near and more near they approach. Slowly the dreamer awakes, and in rapture dwells on the mellow strains. It is the music of the trombone choir that thus early goes forth to usher in the gladsome Easter morn, and with its sweet old chorals gently arouses the slumbering villager, and bids him prepare for the worship of the day. The effect of this ancient custom on the mind surpasses all powers of description. It must be experienced, and then will never be forgotten. The profound stillness of the rural night, unbroken by the clatter of machinery, the roll of wheels, and restless tramp of feet, so absolute and perfect; the clearness and purity of the air at this the most delicious period of the budding spring; the weird and touching sounds of the trombone, so peculiarly adapted to the music of the old chorals; together with the frame of mind induced by the services that have absorbed the attention of the entire previous week, and tended to make the whole soul more exalted and impressionable—all these help to make this part of the Moravian Easter ceremonies striking and beautiful beyond expression."

The Oklahoma *Oberammergau* is an Easter sunrise service based on the traditional passion play, and staged at Holy City in the Wichita Mountains, not far from Lawton. Begun on a modest scale in 1926 by the pastor of the First Congregational Church, it has developed into a great presentation which attracts thousands of interested spectators every year. They begin to gather in the 640-acre tract at sunset on Easter Eve, finding desirable vantage points in the hills overlooking the mammoth natural stage. The setting for the pageant includes replicas of Biblical landmarks such as the inn, the manger, the walls and gates

to the city of Jerusalem. The Judgment Hall, the Upper Room, Calvary, the appropriate settings for the triumphal entry on Palm Sunday, the meeting with Pilate, the Lord's Supper, and the Crucifixion are a part of the permanent background. Each year, the six-hour pageant is an unforgettable experience, despite the uncertainties of the weather. Those who attend bring with them all the equipment needed to keep comfortable in the cold spring air.

In 1921, the Garden of the Gods at Colorado Springs first became the setting for an annual Easter sunrise service. Music predominates at this assembly, and frequently the 300-voice *a cappella* choir of Colorado Springs High School participates. Attendance has increased greatly over the years.

One of the most elaborate sunrise services in America is staged at the Hollywood Bowl in Hollywood, California. It was first started forty years ago, and each year the overflow crowd increases by thousands. They begin to gather at midnight on Easter Eve, in the subdued light of the amphitheater. Thousands of calla lilies are massed in front of the band shell. A "living cross" of 250 teenagers, a choir of 100 adults, an organist, and a symphony orchestra take their places on the stage shortly after dawn. Girl trumpeters, strategically placed, open the program of music, prayers, and sermon. Special features vary from year to year.

A most unusual Easter service, sponsored by five hundred Aztec Indians, is held near San Diego. Mounted on horses, they gather in Alvarado Canyon to greet the sunrise with song, assisted by a trumpeter. At dawn on Easter morning, an impressive program, inaugurated in 1935, is broadcast annually from Grand Canyon National Park. Amid the splendor of the myriad tints of pink and gold, a radio announcer for a national network describes the service, composed of hymns, prayers, Scripture reading, and a brief sermon.

Mountain ranges and craters, historic sites, public parks, college campuses, ancient landmarks, village squares and city plazas have become centers for these observances in recent years. No community church is so small that it has not organized a group of enthusiastic participants to hold an Easter sunrise service. Thus, another age-old folk tradition has become a part of our American heritage.

Reaching out into the Atlantic Ocean, the State of Maine becomes the official greeter of Easter dawn as worshipers gather to watch the sunrise from Cadillac Mountain, the easternmost pinnacle of the United States. The entire state of Maine is the sunrise country of America. The latest ceremony on the mainland of America is held at Yosemite National Park, because of the time required for the sun to rise above the 5000-foot Half Moon Dome so that it can shine on Mirror Lake. At dawn in Tampa, Florida, thirty-three white pigeons are released, signifying the years of Christ's life on earth. Lincoln's birthplace in Hodgenville, Kentucky, serves as the setting for a service while in Utah the most spectacular service is held on the steps of the Capitol at Salt Lake City. At Rindge, New Hampshire, the widely known Cathedral of the Pines forms one of the most impressive backdrops in all New England to salute the sun on Easter morning. And as sunrise comes to the Pacific, the Hawaiians in Honolulu gather for their salutation in the Punchbowl National Memorial Cemetery.

These sunrise services, typical of the Easter morning gatherings all across America, had their origin in the Middle Ages when joyful voices, the shooting of cannons, and the ringing of bells all helped to announce to the world that Christ was risen, as He truly said.

For centuries the eternal spirit of hope, symbolized in the most ancient of all images, the rising of the sun, has left its imprint on many a heart. At Easter, the symbolism becomes all the more meaningful as we commemorate the Resurrection of Our Saviour and its significances, and this eternal truth repeats itself in every sunrise. On a summer morning in 1893, Katharine Lee Bates, a New England schoolteacher, had a profound experience as she viewed the sunrise from Pike's Peak, Colorado. There, standing as close to heaven as any mortal could, she contemplated what she had seen in the world of her day. America—the melting pot of the nations, welding together men and women of all races and creeds, their ideals, customs, traditions and beliefs—symbolized a growing spirit of brotherhood such as no nation had ever achieved.

On that very day she wrote the hymn, "America the Beautiful," which has become known and loved the wide world over—a hymn that is a humble prayer, echoing the commandment given at the Last Supper—to love one another.

> "O beautiful for spacious skies,
> For amber waves of grain,
> For purple mountain majesties
> Above the fruited plain!
> America! America!
> God shed his grace on thee,
> And crown thy good with brotherhood
> From sea to shining sea."

From the collection of Messrs Wartski, London.

(Above) A Fabergé egg of red gold enameled in translucent lime yellow with a green gold laurel leaf trellis. It served as a case for a replica of the Imperial coach used in 1896 at the coronation of Nicholas and Alexandra at Moscow.

(Left) Fabergé jeweled egg of pink enamel quartered by rose diamonds. Lilies of the valley are fashioned of pearls and rose diamonds with leaves of green gold and green enamel.

Collection of Messrs Wartski, London.

Stories of Easter

THE SUGAR EGG

By Carolyn Sherwin Bailey

There was a very important proclamation on the gate of the king's palace, and this was what it said:

"The king wishes a new and different kind of Easter egg for the prince and the princess. It must be brought to the palace on Easter Eve, and there will be a prize for it if it pleases their royal highnesses. If it is like all the former Easter eggs, the subject who brings it will be banished."

Now whoever heard of anything so absurd? Every one in the kingdom, down to the most humble subject, knew their royal highnesses, the Prince Particular and the Princess Perhaps. Not that those were their real names, but whenever the prince was asked if he liked a new toy or game, he would say, "Oh, not particularly," and then he would turn up his nose.

And if you asked the princess if she would like to play something quite merry, she was very apt to say, "Oh, perhaps," with a toss of her head which meant that she did not care whether she did or not.

Of course, every Easter in the past their royal highnesses had hunted for colored eggs on the palace grounds, and had large chocolate eggs made for them in the palace kitchen, and eaten pheasants' eggs for breakfast on Easter Day. How, in the entire kingdom, would it be possible to hatch a new and different egg for them? It could not be done. All the hens hung their heads in despair, and all the farmers expected to be banished from the kingdom on Easter Monday.

But it was not a place of giving up, and in spite of their being so hard to please, their subjects loved the Prince Particular and the Princess Perhaps. So whoever read that strange proclamation on the palace gate went home with the wish to find just the kind of Easter egg for which the king had asked. And a great many people went to work trying to make one.

It was funny, though, the way in which they went about it.

There was the baker. He decided to put several dozen eggs into a huge, egg-shaped cake, so he whisked them up as light as foam, mixed them with flour and other good things, and made a great cake which he frosted with white to look like the biggest egg ever made. On top he put the royal crest in yellow icing. But what a very indigestible Easter egg this one was!

And there was the toy man. He made a mammoth egg-shaped toy dirigible of white rubber, and large enough for their royal highnesses to take a short trip over the palace tree tops and as far as the sea. It was just like a giant egg, but so costly and made with such pains that the toy man had to neglect carving the little wooden dolls and animals which the peasant boys and girls loved to buy at his shop.

There, also, was the jewel cutter. He cut two clear, white diamonds in the shape of tiny eggs, one for the prince to wear as a pin in his scarf, and the other for the princess to hang on a golden chain about her neck. But they only sparkled and sent out darts of light; to touch, they were as cold as the winter that had just passed.

So on Easter Eve there was a crowd of the king's subjects at the entrance to the palace, each with his or her odd Easter egg. They were carved of wood, and shaped of gold and silver, painted in all the colors of the rainbow, and some of them so large that they had to be drawn in carts up to the gates.

 And on the edge of the crowd came Mother Joy who lived all alone in a tiny cottage on the border of the forest. She had very little comfort of her own, but all the children knew and loved her. Such barley sugar candy sticks as Mother Joy made for them, and she could show them the first young magpies, the first cowslips, and where the fresh cress grew in the brook! But, in spite of this, it was strange that Mother Joy should be here at the gate of the palace on Easter Eve, so poor, and so old. And when people spoke of it, Mother Joy only smiled an odd smile and hid something in her apron.

So all the new and different eggs were taken into the palace throne room to be judged, while the subjects waited outside. But the egg balloon had to be tied to the palace chimney, and everyone was sure that it would take the prize. They waited and waited. Then, suddenly, there came the sound of their royal highnesses laughing more merrily than they ever had before, and everyone was called in to see the prize giving.

Such a surprise! On a purple velvet pillow in the lap of the king, the prince and princess and all the court crowded around it, was a little hollow sugar egg. It had a piece of glass fitted in the end like a fairy window, and inside, made of scraps of colored tissue paper and lace and grasses, there was a wee house, a green meadow with flowers and children at play in it. The spring, as it comes in the country, was there inside the little sugar egg, seen through the fairy window in the end.

"The prize winning egg!" cried the king, holding up the sugar egg. "Their royal highnesses have never been so happy in their lives with any Easter egg before. They want to go right out into the fields and play. Riches and a coronet for the maker!"

And Mother Joy in her apron came up to the throne, for she had known what to bring to the palace on Easter Eve, that little picture of the spring with a fairy window to see it through.

It happened that all the eggs won prizes of one sort and another. But the best of all was the little sugar egg. They became the fashion in the kingdom and we have had them ever since.

THE GOLDEN EGG

By Ivy Bolton

The sun was setting over the city of London in a golden glory, a little dimmed by the haze from the river. There was a freshness of spring in the air and the slender little maid, standing by the Thames, lifted her pale face joyously as the soft breezes fanned a tinge of color into her cheeks. She was neatly dressed, though her shoes were worn and her homespun dress patched as well as her faded hood and cloak.

"Daydreaming, Winnie?" asked a boy's voice, and she turned to see a lad about her own age standing at her side.

"Not so much as enjoying the springtime, Stephen," she answered as she seated herself on a low parapet which overhung the river. "I got through with my weaving and spinning early today and Mother sent me out for a breath of air. It has been so close today in the Fleet. But here one can see the trees bursting into leaf and the flowers on the bank and know that Easter is almost here."

"The day after tomorrow, and on Easter Monday the great egg rolling takes place. Are you going to be able to go out on Richmond Hill with us all, Winnie?"

"Mother says that I may."

"The egg rolling is going to be in Master Oglethorpe's grounds, and he is giving a big prize, Winnie. There is going to be hidden a golden egg, and they say it will be worth fifty guineas. Think of the luck of getting that!"

"Oh, if I only could!" She clasped her hands. "I think I would be willing almost to give my life for those fifty guineas."

"What do you want them for so badly?" He looked at her curiously.

She choked back a little sob. "For my father, Stephen. You—you know he is in the Debtors' Prison and he has been there for seven of my thirteen years. Of course, he has to bide in the prison itself, and we live in that little house in the Debtors' Ward. I do not remember much else, only once a big green field when I was a baby and lovely yellow cowslips which Mother made into balls and threw to me."

"You poor little wench." He patted her hand awkwardly. "Do not cry, Winnie. Perhaps your father will get free some day."

"If I could get the golden egg, perhaps he would. It was only fifty guineas that sent him to prison and it was no fault of his that he got into debt. He borrowed it first when Mother was ill, and he had the money all ready to pay it back when it was stolen. That is what has hurt so. The creditor was so angry and he called Father a cheat and said he had hidden the money himself, and then he put him in prison. Father cannot earn anything in prison, and Mother and I can only make enough to feed ourselves and Martin."

"I hope you win it, Winnie. I will help you if I can. It would be wonderful if your father could get out and you could go away from the Fleet back to the country again."

"It would mean so much." She smiled radiantly. "Martin does not remember the green fields at all. You see he was only one year old. Then there is Mother. She had such rosy cheeks and she was always laughing, and now she is thin and pale and so tired all the time. Thank you, Stephen." She rose and he watched her out of sight.

Stephen Mellett had run across Winifred Cheatham in strange fashion. His pet dog had disappeared and he had sought it far and wide. Then one day he saw it following a maid along the Cheap and the two had turned into the Fleet. The boy had followed and the dog, catching sight of his master, had fawned upon him. The girl had spoken joyously.

"Why, he must be yours," she had said. "I found him with a broken leg close by the Thames and I brought him home. Mother set it, and he is almost well now. I am so glad you have found him."

Their friendship dated from that afternoon. Winifred had refused a reward and Stephen had often longed to find some way of serving her.

"You had better do the hiding, Randolph," a grave voice said, and the boy saw two men approaching. They did not notice him below the bank. He recognized the speaker as James Oglethorpe, whose great estate was to be the scene of the festivity on Easter Monday. His companion was unknown to the lad.

"Where shall I hide it?" Randolph asked. "It must be well concealed, for we shall have half of London out with such a prize as this."

"You remember the great oak tree at the left of the tower?" James Oglethorpe said. "In that is an old owl's nest which was my boyhood's hidie hole. Put it there and it will take a clever lad or lass to find it. The egg rolling will be in front and I have planned a good meal to be served in the great hall afterward."

"You love your poor, Oglethorpe."

"Aye, I want to do something for them. I am hoping to be able to help some. I have my Charter, Randolph, to a large tract of land south of the Carolinas in the New World. I hope to transport some of my poor thither."

They passed on and Stephen sat thinking. Here was a clue for Winnie. Surely between them, they could find the great oak and the owl's nest. He looked at the

111

sun. He would have time to go down to the Fleet and find her.

Winifred made her way home slowly. Her heart was light now. Surely she would be able to find the golden egg. If she only could—there was no one in London to whom it would mean more. She stole into the Church of St. Mary-le-Bow opposite to Newgate prison and went into a shadowy corner. The rays of the sunset came through a stained glass window and she raised her face to the Divine One pictured there, a Face which seemed to smile at her.

"Please Thee, Lord," she prayed, "let me find the golden egg. Thou knowest how long Father has been in prison. Thou knowest how lovely are the fields and home—and Martin has never seen them, Lord. Please let me find the egg and set them free. Amen."

She rose and went on her way again. Surely the Lord of the children would hear and help.

"Winnie!" She turned at Stephen's call and he ran to her, excited and flushed. "I have the greatest news," he burst out. "Master Oglethorpe himself came by just after you went, and I heard just where the egg will be hidden. It is to be in the owl's nest in the big oak tree near the tower. We will go right there, Winnie, and just as soon as the signal is given, we will get it."

He ran off without waiting for her reply, and she stood looking after him with a light in her eyes. Why, Our Lord had answered almost before she had finished her prayer, she thought. With happy heart, she lifted the latch of her home and went in.

"You are late, little daughter." Her mother looked up from her work. "I have to finish this sewing for Dame Gurden tonight, so you must get the supper. It is a good one tonight, for Mistress Pettigill has sent in one of her great loaves, and there is a big bowl of milk for each of us as well. Master Hendricks had some left over and he gave me just double. How kind folks are!"

"That is true, Mother." Winnie was spreading the worn checked cloth on the table and setting out pewter spoons and bowls. "Mother, would it not be wonderful if we could go to the country again and live there in a wee cottage with Father?"

Mistress Cheatham sighed. "Wonderful indeed, my maid. But it is a long way off for us I fear. Fifty guineas is a huge sum for those who can make but a few pence a day. But we will go on hoping, and your father never loses courage."

Winifred smiled. "And I will go on hoping too," she said half aloud.

Martin looked up from his horned primer in the corner. "What does h-o-n-o-r-a-b-l-e spell, Winnie?" he asked.

He was a fair-haired little lad with a small pinched face and great wistful grey eyes that seemed all too big for it. Winnie went over to him.

"Honorable, little brother," she said. "What a big word it is."

"And what does it mean?"

"Being honest and truthful and—oh, just not able to do a mean thing."

"I see." He nodded his head. "It is more than being just truthful; it is not taking advantage, like the old knights you tell me about." He looked puzzled. "Is it right to listen and take advantage, Winnie? A boy told me it was all right, but I do not think it was honorable, was it?"

"It is not; why of course it could not be—"

"What is the matter, Winnie? Why are you so white?"

"It—it is nothing—" Winifred stammered. "Supper is ready, Martin. Come, Mother."

She choked down her supper somehow. This was nothing she wanted her mother to see. It was something she must fight out first. She went about her usual duties and saw Martin started for bed. At last she lay down on her own little pallet in the corner of the living room, but not to sleep. Things were too tragic for that.

Would it be wrong to use her knowledge and find the golden egg? Oh, surely it would not be. The golden egg just meant added pleasures for the others; to her it meant everything—home, love, perhaps even the lives of those she loved. Her mother's strength was failing; Martin was frail indeed and this court by the Fleet was airless and cheerless and no place for a child.

"Dear Lord, please let me use it," she prayed again and again.

But her conscience would not rest and at last she dropped into an uneasy sleep.

"You look tired, child," her mother said at the breakfast table. "Have you not slept?"

Winnie went over and put her arms about her lovingly. "Not very well," she owned. "May I go over and speak to Father today?"

"He will be out in the yard now. Go before you begin work; the air will do you good, little daughter."

Winnie donned her cloak. The guard knew her well and smiled at her as he let her into the prison precincts. There, near the iron grating where the debtors' purses hung—to beg a few pence from the passers-by—she saw her father. He never hung his purse up. "We have not begged yet," he told his wife, and it was his own idea to sit and watch the purses of the others. He was whittling now with clever fingers. He raised his haggard face, and his lips broke into a smile as he saw Winnie. He showed her his work.

"It is a boat for Martin," he said. "You can take him to the Heath and he can sail it in the pond there."

"He will love that." She sat down beside him, and he looked at her wistful eyes.

"Are you worrying, my maid? Is anything wrong?" he asked.

"Nothing is wrong; it is just something I cannot decide," she said. "Father, I came to ask your advice. Is it never right to do something—well, just a little dishonorable, if there is a lot involved?"

"No, my maid. You ought to be able to answer that for yourself."

"I ought, but I cannot." Her eyes filled. "If there was a lot involved—if it meant freedom for you, Father, and happiness for us all—would it be so very wrong to take an advantage?"

He put an arm about her, and she leaned an aching head on his shoulder.

"Little daughter, I would rather die in a Debtors' Prison than have you even a shade dishonorable," he said. "But you have answered the question for yourself. You knew it was wrong or you would not have asked the question, and I know you well enough to know you will choose aright. I am proud of my maid."

She blinked back the tears. "You shall not be ashamed of me," she whispered. "I must go back and help Mother now."

It was almost dusk before she was able to go out again, and she went slowly to the Church of St. Mary-le-Bow. Into its coolness she went and knelt in her corner again.

"Dear Lord, I am giving it up," she said aloud. "I cannot ask You for the golden egg now—but O Lord, please help me somehow."

She rose and slipped out. Stephen came up to her.

"What is the matter, Winnie?"

She smiled. "It is just that we cannot take the golden egg, Stephen," she said. "You see they did not know you heard. It would not be honorable."

"I—I had not thought of that—" he faltered. "O Winnie, does it mean you have to give it up?"

She nodded. "It is all right; we just have to give it up," she said bravely. "I am going, Stephen, for Martin wants the fun."

"I will be there, too, and I will see that he gets it, Winnie," Stephen promised.

Easter Monday dawned bright and clear, and Stephen joined Winnie and Martin as they came out at Richmond. Master Oglethorpe's mansion was a quaint Elizabethan one and the great park stretched far around it. There the dappled deer strayed, a little alarmed now as the laughing bands of children ran through, up to the great house. There they were marshalled into lines, and the

breathless hush came as James Oglethorpe explained his plan.

The egg rolling began and the hunt as well, and the whole scene was a merry one. Stephen took care of Martin, and Winnie slipped away to the shade of a great oak on the left. She could see the other oak by the tower and the owl's nest well within reach. Her eyes filled and, with a little sob, she buried her face in the soft moss.

"What is the matter? Have you found no eggs, little maid? Why do you not hunt with the rest?"

She raised her tear-stained face and scrambled to her feet as she saw that it was James Oglethorpe himself who was addressing her.

"I—I may not hunt the golden egg, sir," she faltered. "You see I know where it is—over yonder—and, oh, I wanted it so."

The sobs came faster now. James Oglethorpe put an arm about her and seated her beside himself on a big stone bench.

"How did you know?" he asked.

"Stephen overheard you telling Master Randolph where to hide it," Winnie answered. "We knew then we must not hunt it and—"

"Why do you want it so much?"

"For my father. He—he has been in Debtors' Prison for seven years now—and we cannot earn fifty guineas, Mother and I."

He looked at her little workworn hand. "I think you and Mother may toil overhard," he said. "You are an honorable little maid."

A tall boy came up waving the golden egg. "Well, lad, so you found it? May it bring you good luck."

"It will, sir," the boy answered joyously. "I can go to the Bluecoat School now."

"It is time that we had our supper," James Oglethorpe said. "Come, Giles, and you, Winifred Cheatham. Is that the name?" We must call them all to the feast."

"I am glad you got it," Winifred said shyly to the tall boy. "I hope you are happy in the Bluecoat School."

"I am coming to see your mother sometime," James Oglethorpe said as he bade her farewell. He watched her as she trudged off with Martin.

She was not at home when he came and it was near the river that she met him.

"I have been to see your father, Winifred," he said. "He will be free tomorrow. We have struck a bargain. How would you like to fare forth to the New World, Winnie? To a place where you can make your home and sow great crops and beat a pathway for others to follow? That is what your father has agreed to do. I had not thought of the debtors before, but they are the folk I could help with this new grant of mine.

"He will go with me next month and you all with him. Your friend Stephen is going, too. I had made the arrangement with his family some months agone. Are you happy, little maid? No, do not kiss my hand, but hold out your own."

He took it himself and placed in it something oval and smooth and shining.

"This is your golden egg," he said. "It will make a fairing for you."

"I—I don't know how to thank you," Winnie faltered.

"Your happy eyes do that," he said as he turned away.

Clutching her golden egg, Winnie slipped into the quiet church. "You did find a way," she whispered rapturously. "Oh, I do not know how to thank You. Dear Lord, I love You."

PONCE DE LEON FINDS THE LAND OF FLOWERS

Adapted by WOODBURY LOWERY from
The Spanish Settlements, 1503–1561

In the year 1513 came the famous expedition of Ponce de Leon. The conclusion of the Moorish wars had thrown out of employment a multitude of men, trained in arms and in the endurance of hardships, who swarmed over to the New World, prepared to conquer kingdoms for themselves and their followers. Of such was Juan Ponce de Leon, of noble blood and of one of the most ancient families of Spain.

Ponce had come over to Hispaniola in 1493 with Columbus on his second voyage. Some time later he heard from certain Indians that there was much gold in the neighboring island of Puerto Rico, and obtained leave to visit the island and to search for its wealth. In 1508 he crossed over to Puerto Rico in a small caravel and found many rich treasure rivers. Because of his discoveries he was appointed governor of the island, but he was not destined to remain long in command, for the king removed him from his office. Ponce found himself out of employment, but well provided with means, and with a still undaunted resolution to increase his possessions and extend his estate.

Ponce had heard of an island called Bimini, lying to the north of Hispaniola, in which there was reputed to be a spring of such marvelous virtue that all who drank of its waters were restored to youth and vigour. Here, then, was an opportunity for the scarred and battered warrior, fountains that would infuse young blood into his veins, gold that could be added to his already well-filled coffers, and lands peopled with willing subjects and obedient slaves. So Ponce, employing what influence he had at Court, obtained of Charles V a patent granting him the jurisdiction over the island for all his life.

On Tuesday, the 3d of March, 1513, Ponce set sail from the port of San German in Puerto Rico, taking with him Anton de Alaminos, a native of Palos, as pilot. The following night he stood away north-west by north and continued for eleven days sailing among the Lucayos, as the Bahamas were then called, until on the fourteenth of the same month he reached Guanahani, the San Salvador of Columbus's first landing, where he refitted a ship to cross the bay to the windward of the islands. From thence he steered northwest, and on Easter Sunday, the Spanish *Pasqua de Flores*, the 27th of March, he saw an island and passed it by. The three following days he held on in the same direction, when, the weather proving foul, he changed his course to west-north-west until Saturday the 2d of April, when, having reached a depth of nine fathoms at a distance of a league from land, for the water had grown shoal, he ran along the coast in search of a harbour and anchored at night in eight fathoms of water.

Beyond the shallowing green waters the waves rolled their white crests of foam up the long, hard, shell-paved beaches which formed a silver bar between the sea and the dense green verdure of the islands along which he was coasting. A thick forest of gray cypress, tulip, ash, and magnolia, with gnarled live-oak that reminded the strangers of the olive groves of their native land, clad the low sand-dunes and marshes of the islands and cut the horizon with its dark canopy, above which floated the plumes of towering palm groves and the light tufts of the broom-pine. Between the islands the eye rested upon the glistening surface of sluggish lagoons, with brilliant borders of rush and sedge extending up

to the very edge of the mysterious forest on the mainland.

It was the season of flowers. The perfumed breath of the white lily was wafted out to them from its humid haunts in the shady nooks of the islands; the fragrance of blooming orange groves, of sweet bays, of yellow jasmin, and of the sweet azalea filled the air. Upon the dark foliage, like flights of gaudy butterflies, lay spread masses of blue, crimson, and white, the blue flowers and coral berries of the *Lycium salsum*, the andromeda and the azalea; along the inner shore, between the water's edge and the forest, the royal palmetto, crested with pyramids of silver-white blossoms, thrust forth its sword-shaped leaves. Loons and Spanish curlews whirled overhead; in the woods strutted the wild turkey, saluting the dawn with noisy call from his perch on the lofty cypress or the magnolia, and many-hued humming-birds fluttered from flower to flower.

On some day between the 2d and 8th of April Ponce de Leon went ashore to get an interpreter and take possession. Impressed with its beauty and pleasant groves, and believing it to be an island, he named the land Florida, because he had discovered it at Easter-tide—the Easter of Flowers.

Of the attendant ceremony there is no record. Perhaps, on landing, clad in his battered armour, Ponce offered the simple prayer said to have been used by Columbus, and from whose lips he may have learned it. And then, grasping in his left hand the unfurled banner of Castile and Leon, and with drawn sword in his right, he planted the royal standard upon the soil and proclaimed in a loud voice to the unheeding oaks and palms and to the attendant crews of his caravels the seizure of the land in the name of his king, while he called upon all present to bear witness to his act.

At last they resolved to return to Hispaniola and Puerto Rico. On his way back, Ponce evidently retraced part of his former course through the Florida Keys. Ranging back and forth until the 23d of September, Ponce refitted his ships, and sent one of them under the command of Ortubia, with Anton de Alaminos as pilot, in search of the island of Bimini while he himself returned to Puerto Rico where he was subsequently joined by Ortubia with the caravel, who had discovered the island in search of which he had been sent, but not the wonderful rejuvenating spring reputed to be in it.

Thus ended the first attempt of the Spaniards to reconnoitre and possess the coasts of North America.

A HANDFUL OF CLAY

By Henry van Dyke

There was a handful of clay in the bank of a river. It was only common clay, coarse and heavy; but it had high thoughts of its own value, and wonderful dreams of the great place which it was to fill in the world when the time came for its virtues to be discovered.

Overhead, in the spring sunshine, the trees whispered together of the glory which descended upon them when the delicate blossoms and leaves began to expand, and the forest glowed with fair, clear colours, as if the dust of thousands of rubies and emeralds were hanging, in soft clouds, above the earth.

The flowers, surprised with the joy of beauty, bent their heads to one another, as the wind caressed them, and said: "Sisters, how lovely you have become. You make the day bright."

The river, glad of new strength and rejoicing in the unison of all its waters, murmured to the shores in music, telling of its release from icy fetters, its swift flight from the snow-clad mountains, and the mighty work to which it was hurrying—the wheels of many mills to be turned, and great ships to be floated to the sea.

Waiting blindly in its bed, the clay comforted itself with lofty hopes. "My time will come," it said. "I was not made to be hidden forever. Glory and beauty and honour are coming to me in due season."

One day the clay felt itself taken from the place where it had waited so long. A flat blade of iron passed beneath it, and lifted it, and tossed it into a cart with other lumps of clay, and it was carried far away, as it seemed, over a rough and stony road. But it was not afraid, nor discouraged, for it said to itself: "This is necessary. The path to glory is always rugged. Now I am on my way to play a great part in the world."

But the hard journey was nothing compared with the tribulation and distress that came after it. The clay was put into a trough and mixed and beaten and stirred and trampled. It seemed almost unbearable. But there was consolation in the thought that something very fine and noble was certainly coming out of all this trouble. The clay felt sure that, if it could only wait long enough, a wonderful reward was in store for it.

Then it was put upon a swiftly turning wheel, and whirled around until it seemed as if it must fly into a thousand pieces. A strange power pressed it and moulded it, as it revolved, and through all the dizziness and pain it felt that it was taking a new form.

Then an unknown hand put it into an oven, and fires were kindled about it—fierce and penetrating—hotter than all the heats of summer that had ever brooded upon the bank of the river. But through all, the clay held itself together and endured its trials, in the confidence of a great future. "Surely," it thought, "I am intended for something very splendid, since such pains are taken with me. Perhaps I am fashioned for the ornament of a temple, or a precious vase for the table of a king."

At last the baking was finished. The clay was taken from the furnace and set down upon a board, in the cool air, under the blue sky. The tribulation was passed. The reward was at hand.

Close beside the board there was a pool of water, not very deep, nor very clear, but calm enough to reflect, with impartial truth, every image that fell upon it. There, for the first time, as it was lifted from the board, the clay saw its new shape, the reward of all its patience and pain, the consummation of its hopes —a common flower-pot, straight and stiff, red and ugly. And then it felt that it was not destined for a king's house, nor for a palace of art, because it was made without glory or beauty or honour; and it murmured against the unknown maker, saying, "Why hast thou made me thus?"

Many days it passed in sullen discontent. Then it was filled with earth, and something—it knew not what—but something rough and brown and dead-looking was thrust into the middle of the earth and covered over. The clay rebelled at this new disgrace. "This is the worst of all that has happened to me, to be filled with dirt and rubbish. Surely I am a failure."

But presently it was set in a greenhouse, where the sunlight fell warm upon it, and water was sprinkled over it, and day by day as it waited, a change began to come to it. Something was stirring within it—a new hope. Still it was ignorant, and knew not what the new hope meant.

One day the clay was lifted again from its place, and carried into a great church. Its dream was coming true after all. It had a fine part to play in the world. Glorious music flowed over it. It was surrounded with flowers. Still it could not understand. So it whispered to another vessel of clay, like itself, close beside it, "Why have they set me here? Why do all the people look toward us?"

And the other vessel answered, "Do you not know? You are carrying a royal sceptre of lilies. Their petals are white as snow, and the heart of them is like pure gold. The people look this way because the flower is the most wonderful in the world. And the root of it is in your heart."

Then the clay was content, and silently thanked its maker, because, though an earthen vessel, it held so great a treasure.

THE GENERAL'S EASTER BOX

By Temple Bailey

The General did not look at all as one would expect a general to look. He was short and thick-set and had a red face and a white mustache, and he usually dressed in a gray tweed suit, with a funny Norfolk jacket with a belt, and wore a soft cap pulled down almost to his eye-glasses.

And he always did his own marketing. That is how he came to know Jimmy.

Jimmy stood at a corner of Old Market and sold little bundles of dried sage and sweet marjoram, and sassafras and cinnamon, and soup-bunches made of bits of vegetables tied together—a bit of parsley and a bit of celery and a bit of carrot and a sprig of summer savory, all for one cent. Then at Christmas-time he displayed wreaths, which he and his little mother made at home, and as the spring came on he brought wild flowers that he picked in the woods.

And that was how he came to know the General.

For one morning, just before Easter, the General came puffing down the outside aisle of Old Market, with his colored man behind him with an enormous basket. The General's carriage was drawn up to the curbstone, and the gray horses were dancing little fancy dances over the asphalt street, when all at once Jimmy thrust a bunch of arbutus under the General's very nose.

"Go away, go away," said the General, and trotted down to the carriage door, which a footman held open for him.

But a whiff of fragrance had reached him, and he stopped.

"How much?" he asked.

"Three cents," said Jimmy, in a hoarse voice.

The General looked at the little fellow through his eye-glasses.

"Got a cold?" he inquired gruffly.

"Yes, sir," croaked Jimmy.

"Why don't you stay in the house, then?" growled the General.

"Can't, sir," said Jimmy, cheerfully; "business is business."

The General looked at the little stand where "business" was transacted—at the little rows of dried stuffs, at the small basket of flowers, and at the soup-bunches.

"Humph," he said.

Then his hand went down into his pocket, and he pulled out a lot of change. After that he chose two bunches of sweet, pinky blossoms.

"Two for five, sir," said Jimmy.

"Hum," said the General. "You might give me some parsley and a soup-bunch."

Jimmy wrapped up the green stuff carefully and dropped it into the basket carried by the colored man.

"Nine cents, sir," he said; and the General handed him a dime and then moved to the next stall, holding the flowers close to his nose.

"You forgot your change," cried Jimmy, and rushed after him with the one cent.

"Keep—" But one look at the honest little face and he changed his sentence.

"Thank you, young man," he said, and away he drove.

After that Jimmy looked for the General, and the General for Jimmy. Their transactions were always carried on in a strictly business manner, although, to be sure, the General's modest family of two did not require the unlimited sage and sweet marjoram that were ordered from time to time.

On the Saturday before Easter the little stand was gay with new wares. In little nests of dried grasses lay eggs—Easter eggs, bright pink and blue and purple and mottled. Jimmy had invested in a dozen at forty cents the dozen, and he had hopes of doubling the money, for work surely counted for something, and he and the Little Mother had dyed them.

But somehow the people passed them by. Inside of the market there were finer nests, and eggs gilded and lettered, and Jimmy began to feel that his own precious eggs were very dull indeed.

But when the General appeared around the corner, the boy's spirits rose. Here, at any rate, was a good customer.

The General, however, was in a temper. There had been an argument with the fish-man which had left him red in the face and very touchy. So he bought two bunches of arbutus and nothing else.

"Any eggs, sir?" asked Jimmy.

"Eggs?" said the General, looking over the little stand.

"Easter eggs," explained Jimmy.

"I've no use for such things," said the General.

"Oh!" said Jimmy, and in spite of himself his voice trembled. When one is the man of the family, and the Little Mother is sewing for dear life, and her work and the little stand in the market are all that pay the rent and buy food, it is sometimes hard to be brave. But the General did not notice the tremble.

Jimmy tried again:

"Any children, sir? Children always like Easter eggs, you know."

"No," said the General; "no one but a son in the Philippines—a son some six feet two in his stockings."

"Any grandchildren, sir?" hopefully.

"Bless my soul," said the General, testily, "what a lot of questions!" And he hurried off to his carriage.

Jimmy felt very forlorn. The General had been his last hope. The eggs were a dead loss.

At last it came time to close up, and he piled all of his wares in a basket. Then he took out a little broom and began to sweep in an orderly way around his little stall. He had a battered old dustpan, and as he carried it out to the street to empty it, he saw a stiff greenish gray paper sticking out of the dirt. Nothing in the world ever looks exactly like that but an American greenback, and, sure enough, when Jimmy pulled it out it proved to be a ten-dollar bill.

Jimmy sat down on the curb suddenly. His money always came in pennies and nickels and dimes and quarters. The Little Mother sometimes earned a dollar at a time, but never in his whole life had Jimmy possessed a ten-dollar bill.

Think of the possibilities to a little, poor, cold, worried boy. There was two months' rent in that ten-dollar bill—two months in which he would not have to worry over whether there would be a roof over their heads.

Then there was a basket stall in that ten-dollar bill. That had always been his ambition. Some one had told him that baskets sold well in other cities, and not a single person had opened a basket stall in Old Market, and that was Jimmy's chance. Once established, he knew he could earn a good living.

As for ten dollars' worth of groceries and provisions, Jimmy's mind could not grasp such a thing; fifty cents had always been the top limit for a grocery bill.

But—it wasn't Jimmy's ten dollars. Like a flash his dreams tumbled to the ground. There had been many people coming and going through Old Market, but Jimmy knew that the bill was the General's. For the old gentleman had pulled out a roll when he reached for the five cents. Yes, it was the General's; but how to find the General?

Inside the market he found the General's butcher. Yes, the butcher knew the General's address, for he was one of his

119

best customers, and would keep Jimmy's basket while the boy went to the house.

It was a long distance. Jimmy passed rows of great stone mansions, and went through parks, where crocuses and hyacinths were just peeping out.

At last he came to the General's.

A colored man answered the ring of the bell.

"Who shall I say?" he inquired loftily. "The General is very busy, y'know."

"Say Jimmy, from the market, please"; and Jimmy sat down on the great hall seat, feeling very much awed with all the magnificence.

"Well, well," said the General, as he came puffing down the stairs. "Well, well, and what do you want?"

"Please, sir, did you drop this?" and Jimmy held out the tightly rolled bill.

"Did I? Well, now, I'm sure I don't know. Perhaps I did, perhaps I did."

"I found it in front of my stall," said Jimmy.

What a strange thing it seemed that the General should not know! Jimmy would have known if he had lost a penny. He began to feel that the General could not have a true idea of *business*.

The General took out a roll of bills. "Let me see," he said. "Here's my market list. Yes, I guess that's mine, sure enough."

"I'm glad I noticed it," said Jimmy, simply. "I came near sweeping it into the street."

"And what can I pay you for your trouble?" asked the General, looking at the boy keenly.

"Well," said Jimmy, stoutly, "you see, business is business, and I had to take my time, and I'd like to get back as soon as I can."

The General frowned. He was afraid he was going to be disappointed in this boy. What, after all, if he was a beggar—

"And so," went on Jimmy, "if you would give me a nickel for car-fare, I think we might call it square."

The General fumbled around for his eye-glasses, put them on, and looked at Jimmy in astonishment.

"A nickel?" he asked.

"Yes, sir." Jimmy blushed. "You know, I ought to get back."

"Well, well," said the General. The boy had certainly the instincts of a gentleman. Not a single plea of poverty, and yet one could see that he was poor, very poor.

Just then a gong struck softly somewhere. "I'm not going to let you go until you have a bit of lunch with us," said the General. "I have told my wife of Jimmy of the market, and now I want you to meet her."

So Jimmy went down into a wonderful dining-room, where the silver and the cut glass shone, and where at the farther side of the table was the sweetest little old lady, who came and shook hands with him.

Jimmy had never before eaten lunch where the soup was served in little cups, but the General's wife put him at his ease when she told him that his very own soup-bunches were in that soup, and if he didn't eat plenty of it he wouldn't be advertising his wares. Then the General, with knife upraised, stopped in his carving of the cold roast chicken, and turned to Jimmy with a smile of approval in his genial face, and said that it was his sage, too, that was in the chicken dressing.

They made Jimmy talk, and finally he told them of his ambition for a basket stall.

"And when do you expect to get it?" asked the General, with a smile.

"When I get the goose that lays the golden egg, I am afraid, sir," said Jimmy, a little sadly.

Then the General's wife asked questions, and Jimmy told her about the Little Mother, and of their life toegther; but not one word did he tell of their urgent need, for Jimmy had not learned to beg.

At last the wonderful lunch was over, somewhat to Jimmy's relief, it must be confessed.

"I shall come and see your mother, Jimmy," said the General's wife, as Jimmy left her.

Out in the hall the General handed the boy a nickel. "Business is business, young man," he said, with a twinkle in his eye.

That night Jimmy and his mother sat up very late, for the boy had so much to tell

"Do you think I was wrong to ask for the nickel, Mother?" he asked anxiously, when he had finished.

"No," said his mother, "but I am glad you didn't ask for more."

Then, after Jimmy had gone to bed, the mother sat up for a long time, wondering how the rent was to be paid.

On Easter Monday morning Jimmy and the Little Mother started out to pick the arbutus and the early violets which Jimmy was to sell Tuesday at his little stall.

It was a sunshiny morning. The broad road was hard and white after the April showers, the sky was blue, and the air was sweet with the breath of bursting buds. And, in spite of cares, Jimmy and his mother had a very happy time as they filled their baskets.

At last they sat down to tie up the bunches. Carriage after carriage passed them. As the last bunch of flowers was laid in Jimmy's basket, a victoria drawn by a pair of grays stopped in front of the flower-gatherers.

"Well, well," said a hearty voice, and there were the General and his wife! They had called for Jimmy and his mother, they said, and had been directed to the wooded hill.

"Get in, get in," commanded the General; and, in spite of the Little Mother's hesitancy and timid protests, she was helped up beside the General's wife by the footman, while Jimmy hopped in beside the General, and away they went over the hard white road.

The General was in a gay mood.

"Well, my boy, have you found your golden egg?" he asked Jimmy.

"No, sir," said Jimmy, gravely; "not yet."

"Too bad, too bad," said the old gentleman, while he shifted a white box that was on the seat between himself and Jimmy to the other side.

"You're quite sure, are you, that you could only get it from a goose?" he asked later.

"Get what, sir?" said Jimmy, whose eyes were on the gay crowds that thronged the sidewalks.

"The egg," said the General.

"Oh—yes, sir," replied Jimmy, with a smile.

The General leaned back and laughed and laughed until he was red in the face; but Jimmy could see nothing to laugh at, so he merely smiled politely, and wondered what the joke was.

At last they reached Jimmy's home, and the General helped the Little Mother out. As he did so he handed her a white box. Jimmy was busy watching the gray horses, and saw nothing else.

"For the boy," whispered the General, The Little Mother shook her head doubtfully.

"Bless you, madam," cried the General, testily, "I have a boy of my own— if he *is* six feet two in his stockings." Then, in a softer tone, "I beg of you to take it, madam; it will please an old man and give the boy a start."

So when good-by had been said, and Jimmy stood looking after the carriage and the prancing grays, the Little Mother put the white box in his hand.

Jimmy opened it, and there on a nest of white cotton was an egg. But it was different from any of the eggs that Jimmy had sold on Saturday. It was large and gilded, and around the middle was a yellow ribbon.

Jimmy lifted it out, and found it very heavy.

"What do you think it is?" he said.

"Untie the ribbon," advised his mother, whose quick eyes saw a faint line which showed an opening.

Jimmy pulled the yellow ribbon, the upper half of the egg opened on a hinge, and there, side by side, were glistening gold coins—five-dollar gold pieces, and five of them.

"Oh!" said Jimmy, and he sat down

on the step, breathless with surprise and joy.

A slip of white paper lay between two of the coins. Jimmy snatched it out, and this is what he read:

Please accept the contents of the golden egg, with the best wishes of
THE GOOSE

And then at last Jimmy saw the joke.

YS AND HER BELLS

By Marguerite Clement

Do you know how quaint they are, those folk from Brittany? Now ordinary people, like you and me, enjoy reading or writing about ghosts once in a while. Dear ghosts! Bare-footed, long-robed, leisurely and reserved, they are such a pleasant change from the humans we come across, in the subway! Still, when we are more than, say, nine years old, we no longer take ghosts too seriously, not as seriously as ourselves. They have their little room in our lives, close to the children's corner, and they disturb but little our busy, sensible thoughts.

Not so in Brittany. I suppose it is misty too often over there for people to make such a difference between what they see and what they fancy. Besides, they fancy very beautiful things, which have got a right to be believed in. I told you those people were quaint: they actually meet their dreams alive, walking round the corner.

Not so long ago, for instance, in a small village, by the sea, two girls came home late at night. They were breathless and excited, although not exactly scared. And this is what they said.

They were talking and laughing along that little path which runs by Thomas's field. As a matter of fact, they were talking about the boys making fun of them, for they were young, they were pretty, they thought a lot of themselves and had, as yet, no pity to waste on their humble admirers. They may have laughed a little too loud; they could not tell. Anyway, all of a sudden, an old man, a very old man with sad eyes and a bushy beard, stood there, by their side. They had not heard his footsteps, which was strange. How long had he been following them?

Yes, he had said things, oh! nothing very particular. He had asked them if they were good, if they were happy, if they loved their father, if they were not too fond of dancing. He seemed somewhat afraid of that. And then he had paid them little sad compliments about their rosy cheeks. A good little girl's rosy cheeks, he said, were the only sight which made him forget his grief. . . . No, they had not asked him what grief. Oh! dear, no! He was too sad, don't you see. Also, he was not that sort of a man one dares to ask questions of. He had left them suddenly and noiselessly, before they reached the church, and they did not know where he had gone.

Now, the girls' father did not hesitate a minute. That's the beauty of the story. He knew the ghost right away. "Poor King Gralon," he said, "it's quite a while since he was heard of in this neighborhood! We'd better recite the De Profundis, girls, for the Lord to give peace, at last, to his poor soul."

But will poor King Gralon ever get any peace, considering that he has been roaming over the small paths of Brittany for some fifteen hundred years? Would you like me to tell you his story, the terrible tale of a daughter's wickedness and a father's despair? I believe you ought to know it, though it is so tragic, because it hovers over all the land and sea, over there, strange and glittering like their golden mist. They tell it in many ways. You may even find a few details in my story that are nowhere else. Never mind that. Nobody knows for sure what happened, don't you see, although we are almost certain that some terrible thing, once, did really happen.

How long ago did King Gralon live? I could not tell. Surely very long ago, since the people of Brittany had just been converted to the Christian faith, and not all of them, yet. And so hermits and bishops were very busy working miracles every day, to make the last pagans ashamed of their senseless powerless gods. And they preached a rather austere creed, as you will see. They could not take liberties with the Gospel in those early days. When we read, "If thy hand offend thee, cut it off and cast it from thee," we say it is a metaphor, and it just means we have got to be careful; when we read, "Woe to the rich," we say it means we must not possess too much; and when we read, "Put back thy sword into its scabbard," we say it means we are allowed to make war only when we cannot help it.

But the saintly preacher whom King Gralon knew was not so clever, by far. He accepted and revered, for himself and for his people, every single word of his book. His name was Guénolé, and he had no fear of kings, and he spoke his mind very plainly to Gralon about his daughter Dahut. Several times a year, he would leave his cell, dug out of the rock by the roaring sea, to make a trip to the palace and there deliver his warning.

"Thy daughter is a curse, King. Stop her ways; have her tried by the judges of thine own court. Because it is written, 'If thy heart offend thee, cut out thy heart and cast it from thee.' The wrath of God will visit thy house, King, and thy kingdom, if thou dost not heed His word. Help thyself against thyself, man. Save thy soul."

Gralon would listen and grow pale and kneel down before the holy hermit, but he would not do anything else: Dahut was too precious to him.

He always remembered the day when little Dahut was born, the same day on which his queen died.

And Dahut was so much like her! She had the same glossy braids, the same fathomless eyes. You never could tell what was in her thoughts and, when she sang, it seemed as if the waves themselves made less noise so that they could hear. As for the beauty of her face, after eighteen years, Gralon had not got used to it, and he looked at her every morning with a fresh delight. She made him think of the sun and of the stars and of the sea and of all the joy and of all the sadness of living. Could it be possible that Dahut was wicked at heart, as Guénolé said? Gralon did not dare to think.

Certainly, her ways were strange. Had she been just a sweet coquette, as so many of them are, Gralon would not have worried. But she was not a coquette. She despised all men, except, perhaps, her own father. The idea that one of those boys might become her lord and master made her shiver with cold disdain. They say that, when she was still a little girl, she had betrothed herself to the ocean, as it was the only strong thing which she respected and admired.

Now, such being the case, she might have become a nun, in the quiet convent that Guénolé had just established in one of the wild islands, amid the foam and the fog, and the rocks and the wind. Why did she not go there, to be thrilled by the tempest, to her heart's content, and forget about life and her inhuman contempt of it?

But she did not want to go to the nuns, in the island. Because she was as cruel as she was proud. She wanted men to look at her freely, to fall desperately in love with the glittering beauty of her face, and then to throw themselves down from the cliff, into that abyss which is still called the Devil's Pit, hoping that it would be more merciful to them than those cold, fathomless eyes.

And so, one after the other, for the two past years, all the boys in Gralon's kingdom had followed the same way. It

would take some but a little time; others would resist longer. And when Dahut felt afraid that some young man might escape her power, she would then give a ball in the huge hall by the sea, and she would dance and dance and dance with the rebellious youth until he gave way in his turn and drowned himself early, at dawn, the following morning.

And Dahut would say to her father, "Why, Father, I never promised any of those men anything. Must I be responsible for the foolishness of those weaklings? Or do you want me to go with a veil over my face, like the nuns on the island? I could not, Father. I'd die if I could not look at the sun and the stars and the white waves. And I must look at the boys too, in case I see one whom I might love. I am not doing anything wrong. A girl has her free choice."

And then poor King Gralon would mutter a few indistinct words about the mad dancing in the huge hall by the sea, and Dahut would retort with anger, "Will all the girls in your kingdom be allowed to dance except me, or do you want me to dance by myself?" And then she would sigh and say, "Aren't you tired of it all, anyway, Father? Sometimes I wish that your palace and its huge hall, and your kingdom with its cowardly men, and all of us could be washed away by the strong, splendid sea. I wish I were a white wave, Father, to dance and sing with them forever."

Poor Dahut! There are moments when I feel as if I could pity her, too. She was not made for the Christian faith and the new era. She belonged with the wild things which were dying. It was right for Guénolé to be her mortal enemy.

But what about the mothers and the sweethearts of the men who had gone down? Whenever Dahut strolled along the streets, they closed their doors and put a black curtain across their windows.

And yet Gralon did nothing. And, all in vain, several times a year did Saint Guénolé come out of his cell by the roaring sea, to curse Dahut and threaten her father with the wrath of the Lord.

I have not told you yet the name of Gralon's capital. It was called Ys and lay by the ocean, just below the level of the water, so that they had built an enormous dam to protect the town from the fury of the flood. And the key of the dam was made of pure gold, and it was hidden in a secret place, as the safety of so many depended upon it. The dam was opened but seldom, once a year, perhaps, during a very low tide. Then they would clean the massive wall quickly, for fear the mud and the sand and the shells and the weeds might eat away the stone, little by little. And then they would shut the dam in a great hurry, as the flood rushed in like a galloping horse, and Gralon would hide the key until the following year.

Nobody but he knew where the key was hidden—he and the poor young man whose father had built the dam. Gralon had deemed it safer to tell just one person in case he, the king, died a sudden death, and he had told that one because he was his father's son, a devout, silent youth, and because he was a hunchback, not likely to marry, thought Gralon, nor to attract the attention, the deadly attention of Dahut.

In fact, the hunchback had never looked at her once, having given his love to Ys, his town, to Ys and her hundred spires, where a hundred big bells sang the glory of God louder than the sea. And his name was Gavin, and he was happy all day and all night, because the safety of Ys, the beautiful, depended upon his faith.

And so, of course, it was Gavin whom, one terrible day, at springtime and just before Easter, Dahut, the sorceress, sought along the numberless little streets winding around the gorgeous churches with their dazzling white spires.

She found him alone in a narrow passage which led to the wide sea. She opened her lovely mouth, breathed the salt air, which made her frantic, and called the boy by his name:

"Gavin," she said, "why don't you ever look at me?"

And then Gavin looked at her, but he did not see the wonderful face because of the vision which was in his head: the image of Ys the beautiful, with the hundred bells of its hundred spires, stood like a veil between him and her and protected him.

"Princess Dahut," answered he, "what can I do for your service?" Dahut stood disconcerted. For the first time she had seen neither fear nor love in a man's eyes. She soon recovered though. "Give me the key," she said, "which my father has hidden with thee."

Now, Dahut knew nothing about the key. It was just a new idea which had visited her at night, while she lay wide awake, listening to the clamoring flood and mad with the devilish desire to see it engulf all things, as well as all men. But Gavin was a simple boy. He thought the king had told her, unable as he was to resist any of her demands. And so he grew as pale as Death, and he clutched his fingers over his poor shriveled chest and he said: "Never."

And then Dahut knew. She knew that the key was there, hidden against the faithful heart, and she laughed aloud, a terrible laugh which the sea echoed amid the wild rocks, and the boy crossed himself, aghast but unconquered.

She began wrestling with him. A poor cripple he was, but with all the courage of mankind. For he was a man, and he felt she was not human. She was strong as the wind, slippery as a weed, and cool like the green water. And she smiled while she fought, and her smile was like the golden joy of dawn. But, all the same, Gavin went on fighting. He could not win, of course, but he could be faithful to the end, faithful to Ys and her bells. And, as Death came nearer and nearer, he could hear them all, the hundred bells of the hundred spires, ringing through his dizzy head their great victorious song.

She pushed the dead body into the sea with her foot, and she said, "One more."

She did not want to use the key at once, or perhaps ever. It was enough for her to know that it was there, cool and powerful, close to her wicked heart; enough to feel that *she could do it* the next time she felt tired of men, of bells and of life altogether. She also wondered what Gralon would say when he heard that his dear hunchback had gone the way of all men—not willingly, though. That one had escaped her magic—she could not enslave them all. Guénolé, in his cell, was safe too. . . . How he hated her! . . . "If thy heart offend thee, King, cut out thy heart." . . . She laughed again. So much fuss for a few despicable fishermen whose death had been graced by the memory of her smile! . . . What about the rights of queens, then? If the likes of Guénolé had their way, some day, the world would become a dull place, indeed. . . . A good thing the key was there.

She strolled back to the palace, but her heart was heavy. The recollection of her wrestling with a hunchback was disgusting beyond words. And the look in his eyes was strange, too. What could he behold which was more beautiful than Dahut's face, and what had helped him to die?

She had now been back for a few hours and was sitting with her father in the big hall, by the sea. All of a sudden, it seemed as if the wind had put a few words to its wild tune. Yes—and the words were, "Death to Dahut! Death to Dahut! . . ."

She thought she was feverish; she went and opened the window. . . . "Death to Dahut!" clamored the tempest, which shouted now with a human voice. . . . Down, at the foot of the cliff, a crowd was coming toward the palace, like a living, furious flood. The women were there, waving their black veils like a standard. And the old men were there, flourishing their crutches. And there were little girls and tiny boys who swelled their pure cheeks to try to scream, "Death

to Dahut!" Dahut could see, in front, the dead body of the hunchback, dripping with water, on a bed of seaweed. And he was the only silent and serene figure among that hellish crowd.

. . . "Death to Dahut!" chanted the wind, which seemed to take sides with the mob and make its yelling beautiful. . . . "Death to Dahut!" . . . "Death to Dahut!"

King Gralon was brave. He faced the human tide which was surging against his walls, with stones and sticks and curses.

"What do you want, people?" he said. "Am I no longer your king?"

"Death to Dahut!" answered the crowd. "Deliver her up to our justice, O King! Death to Dahut!"

And Gralon could hear within his conscience, "If thy heart offend thee, cut out thy heart." But he also thought of his dead queen, who had left him nothing except Dahut's eyes. He fancied what an empty place the world would be without them, and he said, "Take me, people. I am ready to pay for her, if you can prove her guilt."

But the mob respected Gralon. They were not seeking vengeance, but justice. And an old man in the crowd exclaimed: "Have her judged, King, by thine own Court."

That was the last word Dahut heard. And then she threw a white cape on her shivering body; she ran to the secret door which led to the huge, massive dam, and she went out and looked at the sky. The watchful moon was there. But Dahut did not mind the moon—the moon which has seen so many cities rise and fall beneath her cold eyes while the joyful sea bounces and leaps, as young as ever, toward the silvery face which she tries to kiss eternally. Of course, the moon was on Dahut's side and Dahut knew it.

The night was clear, although the wind was strong, and she could now hear both the human tide—Death to Dahut!—and the coming flood, charging against the wall of the dam like a despairing army in a desperate fight. Dahut quietly smiled.

She was going to give the beaten one his chance. It took very little time, just one flash upon the shining key, then the massive door glided, unconscious, like a sentry asleep, and, with a roar which disturbed the stars, the whole ocean stood erect, defying Ys, her spires, and her bells, and the vain anger of her mob. And then it thundered down, foaming, into the streets, while the people gave one last scream—a screaming appeal to the Lord.

The Lord did not answer the people of Ys. He received them in His Paradise, I suppose, as soon as they were drowned, for they had done nothing wrong, and they were not responsible for the wickedness of Dahut, and I'll tell you in a moment what the Lord did for Ys and her bells, because He loved the way they sang to His glory.

But, for the time being, the wrath of the Lord visited Gralon and his house, as Saint Guénolé had so often predicted. King Gralon wandered through his halls, sick with despair. His instinct had been to shut the big window, and so he was safe for a little time—the palace stood high and the walls were so thick! But King Gralon did not think of his safety. He knew that Dahut had done it, he knew her soul was lost forever, and he felt no desire to go to heaven where she would never be, or to remain on earth where she was no more. He had loved her better than God and His law, don't you see, better than the poor people committed to his care. But, since his sin had been a sin of love, there was no bitterness in him—nothing except a great fatigue, as if he had carried the burden of every man, ever since man had been. He wanted to sleep until doomsday and, if possible, beyond. And, instead of sleep, who was coming for him but Saint Guénolé holding the king's horse, Morvark, by the bridle! And Guénolé said, "Get up on thy horse and ride, O King! because the Lord needs thee elsewhere." And they went out through the big window, and Morvark galloped on the beach, breast deep in the water, while Guénolé, the man of God. ran on the waves ahead of them, to show the way.

And it was then that the terrible thing happened, that thing which Gralon cannot forget and which keeps him roaming, in his grief, along the paths of Brittany. All of a sudden, Gralon felt as if somebody were clinging to the horse in a desperate effort to climb up. He looked, and he saw Dahut, and at first he did not know her, for the deadly pallor on her face and the ghastly fright in her eyes. She could hardly speak and she could not breathe. She just pointed to the pit—you know—to the Devil's Pit. . . . "There," she said—"there. . . ." And the story said that what she saw there was the procession of all the young men who had died for her. Each wave brought up a new one, and the ghosts beckoned to Dahut from the depths of the sea. And Dahut felt like a woman for the first time in her life, and there was nothing left in her except a savage desire to escape, to get on Morvark's back and taste of life once more.

But Guénolé, too, had turned round; his hour had come and he was unmoved.

"Cast her away, King, where she belongs. It would have been better for all if she had never been born."

"Father," implored Dahut, "I am your only child. I want to stay with you and I am afraid, Father, I am afraid. Don't give me back to them."

And Guénolé repeated, "Cast her away."

"I am like my mother," stammered the terrified girl. "For her sweet sake, let me get up here."

But Guénolé: "Take thy choice between her and God. O King, it is written, 'Cut out thy heart, if thy heart tempt thee.'"

They say that, at this moment, Gralon, too, saw the young men whom the pit was bringing forward, one after the other, to bear witness against his only love, and Morvark, at last, all of a sudden, neighed to heaven and refused to advance farther.

And then—then—Gralon freed himself from Dahut's embrace; Morvark kicked the waves wildly, and the King fell upon the back of his horse, like a dead man, while Guénolé led the two thither, where they were called.

Don't ask me what has become of Dahut, because I am afraid the young men of Brittany are not yet freed from her charm. They hear her sing in the tempest, her glossy braids shine in every sunset, and it is her smile which, in summer, lights up the sea. Despite their mothers' prayers, despite their wives' tears, they all want to join her, amid the merry round of the wild white waves. They all go, sooner or later, and not all of them come back. Dahut is now one with the strong, splendid sea. The people call it, sometimes, by her name.

And although King Gralon became a saintly king, later on, in his new kingdom, although Saint Guénolé would willingly lead him before the throne of God the minute he wants to go, Gralon has not wanted to, yet. He prefers lingering down below, a harmless ghost among the people of Brittany. He converses at twilight with some of their fair daughters, to try to keep them pure, kind, and happy. They say that those narrow paths are so pretty, in spring, when the gorse is in bloom, that Gralon must not be pitied too much, after all.

And on Easter Day—not every year, of course—but when the day is unusually quiet and when the year is going to be a blessed one, if you sit on the rock and try to look through the blue water, as far below as you can see, the spires of Ys the beautiful will rise from the depths, before your wondering eyes.

If there is no sin in your heart, you will even hear the bells, those bells which the Lord liked so much that He has sheltered them down there in the abyss, where they keep ringing forever to Him alone, forever.

H. Armstrong Roberts

Bibliography

ADAMS, CHARLOTTE. *Easter Idea Book.* New York: Barrows, 1954.

ALFORD, VIOLET. *Introduction to English Folklore.* London: Bell, 1952.

ANDERSON, A. W. *The Coming of the Flowers.* New York: Farrar, Straus & Young, 1960.

———. *Plants of the Bible.* New York: Philosophical Library, 1957.

ANON. *The Book of Easter.* New York: Macmillan, 1910.

BAILEY, ALBERT E. *The Gospel in Hymns.* New York: Scribner's, 1950.

BALY, DENIS. *The Geography of the Bible: A Study in Historical Geography.* New York: Harper, 1957.

BARBEAU, MARIUS. *The Golden Phoenix and Other French-Canadian Fairy Tales Retold by Michael Hornyansky.* New York: Walck, 1960.

BAZIN, GERMAIN. *A Gallery of Flowers.* London: Thames-Hudson, 1960.

BEECHING, H. K. *Essays and Studies by Members of the English Association.* Oxford: Clarendon Press, 1911.

BELKNAP, E. MCCAMLY. *Milk Glass.* New York: Crown, 1949.

BRAND, JOHN. *Observations on Popular Antiquities.* London: Chatto & Windus, 1913.

Brewer's Dictionary of Phrase and Fable, Revised and Enlarged. New York: Harper, 1953.

BROOKE, JOSELYN. *The Flower in Spain: A Calendar of Wild Flowers.* London: The Bodley Head.

BROWNE, LEWIS. *This Believing World.* New York: Macmillan, 1926.

CAMP, WENDELL, BOSWELL, VICTOR R., and MAGNESS, JOHN R. *The World in Your Garden.* Washington, D.C.: National Geographic Society, 1957.

CARTER, MORRIS. *Isabel Stewart Gardner and Fenway Court.* Boston: Houghton Mifflin, 1925.

CLAUDE-SALVY. *Quai aux Fleurs.* Paris: Marchot, Librairie Grund, 1952.

COATS, ALICE M. *Flowers and Their Histories.* New York: Pitman, 1956.

COLLINS, ARTHUR H. *Symbolism of Animals and Birds.* London: Pitman, 1913.

COOLIDGE, OLIVIA. *Greek Myths.* Boston: Houghton Mifflin, 1949.

CORCORAN GALLERY OF ART, *Easter Eggs and Other Precious Objects by Carl Fabergé.* Washington, D.C.: The Corcoran Gallery of Art, 1961.

COULTON, G. G. *Medieval Panorama: The English Scene from Conquest to Reformation.* New York: Macmillan, 1947.

DALY, LLOYD W. *Aesop without Morals.* New York: Yoseloff, 1961.
DEARMER, PERCY, WILLIAMS, R. VAUGHAN, and SHAW, MARTIN. *The Oxford Book of Carols.* London: Oxford University Press, 1928.
DYER, T. F. T. *The Folklore of Plants.* New York: Appleton, 1889.
Easter Ideals: An Annual. Milwaukee: Ideals Pub. Co., 1950–1961.
Easter Picture Book. Now at the Victoria and Albert Museum. Her Majesty's Stationery Office, 1952.
Easter Stories for Children. Milwaukee: Ideals Pub. Co., 1960.
EMERY-WATERHOUSE, FRANCES. *Banana Paradise.* New York: Stephen-Paul, 1947.
EVANS, SEBASTIAN. *The High History of the Holy Grail.* New York: Dutton, 1910.
EWING, JULIANA H. *The Peace Egg and a Christmas Mumming Play.* New York: E. & J. B. Young, 1887.
FAISON, S. L., JR. *A Guide to the Art Museums of New England.* New York: Harcourt Brace, 1958.
FENNER, PHYLLIS R. *Feasts and Frolics: Special Stories for Special Days.* New York: Knopf, 1949.
FERGUSON, GEORGE. *Signs and Symbols in Christian Art.* New York: Oxford, 1954.
Festival Poems: A Collection for Christmas—The New Year—Easter. Boston: Roberts, 1884.
FOLEY, DANIEL J. *Little Saints of Christmas.* Boston: Dresser, Chapman & Grimes, 1959.
———. *The Christmas Tree.* Philadelphia: Chilton, 1960.
FRASER, JAMES G., and GASTER, THEODOR H. *The New Golden Bough.* New York: Criterion, 1959.
FRYATT, NORMA R. *A Horn Book Sampler.* Boston: The Horn Book, 1959.
FUSSELL, G. E. and K. R. *The English Countrywoman.* London: Andrew Melrose, 1953.
GASTER, THEODOR H. *Passover: Its History and Traditions.* New York: Schuman, 1949.

GENDERS, ROY. *Perfume in the Garden.* London: Museum Press, 1952.
GOLDIN, HYMAN E. *A Treasury of Jewish Holidays: History, Legends, Traditions.* New York: Twayne, 1952.
GOMBRICH, E. H. *The Story of Art.* New York: Phaidon, 1958.
GOODALL, NAN. *Donkey's Glory.* Philadelphia: McKay, 1959.
GOUDGE, ELIZABETH. *God So Loved the World.* New York: Coward-McCann, 1951.
———. *My God and My All.* New York: Coward-McCann, 1959.
GRIGSON, GEOFFREY. *The Englishman's Flora.* London: Phoenix House, 1955.
GUERBER, H. A. *Legends of the Virgin and Christ.* New York: Dodd, Mead, 1896.
HALE, EDWARD EVERETT. *Easter: A Collection for a Hundred Friends.* Boston: J. Smith, 1886.
HAMILTON, EDITH. *The Greek Way to Western Civilization.* New York: Mentor Books, 1930.
———. *Mythology.* New York: Mentor Books, 1930.
———. *The Roman Way.* New York: Mentor Books, 1932.
HAMILTON, LORD FREDERIC. *The Vanished Pomps of Yesterday.* New York: Doran, 1921.
HARPER, THE REV. HOWARD V., D.D. *Days and Customs of All Faiths.* New York: Fleet, 1957.
HARRINGTON, MILDRED P., and THOMAS, JOSEPHINE H. *Our Holidays in Poetry.* New York: Wilson, 1929.
HARTING, JAMES E. *The Rabbit.* New York: Longmans, Green, 1898.
HASTINGS, JAMES D. D. (ed.). *A Dictionary of Christ and the Gospels.* New York: Scribner's, 1912.
The Herbalist. Hammond, Indiana: Hammond Book Co., 1934.
HEYERDAHL, THOR. *Aku-Aku: The Secret of Easter Island.* Chicago: Rand McNally, 1958.
HOLE, CHRISTINA. *Easter and Its Customs.* New York: Barron, 1961.

HOTTES, ALFRED CARL. *Garden Facts and Fancies*. New York: Dodd, Mead, 1937.

HOWELLS, VICTOR. *A Naturalist in Palestine*. London: Andrew Melrose, 1956.

HUNT, FERN B. *Floral Decorations for Your Church*. Philadelphia: Chilton, 1960.

HUNTINGTON, VIRGINIA. *In Green Autumn*. Philadelphia: Dorrance, 1941.

HUTCHINSON, RUTH, and ADAMS, RUTH. *Every Day's a Holiday*. New York: Harper, 1951.

INMAN, THOMAS, M.D. *Ancient Pagan and Modern Christian Symbolism*. New York: J. W. Bouton, 1884.

JAMES, M. R. *Abbeys*. London: Great Western Railway, 1926.

JENKIN, A. K. H. *Cornish Homes and Customs*. New York: Dutton, 1934.

JONES, WILLIAM. *Credulities Past and Present*. London: Chatto & Windus, 1880.

KANE, HARNETT T. *Queen New Orleans: City by the River*. New York: Morrow, 1949.

KELLER, WERNER. *The Bible as History: A Confirmation of the Book of Books*. Translated by William Neil. New York: Morrow, 1956.

KEYES, FRANCES PARKINSON. *All This Is Louisiana*. New York: Harper, 1950.

KONSTANDT, OSCAR (Tr.). *The Most Beautiful Alpine Flowers*. Innsbruck: Penguin-Verlag, 1957.

KRYTHE, MAYMIE R. *All About American Holidays*. New York: Harper, 1962.

KUBLY, HERBERT. *Easter in Sicily*. New York: Simon & Schuster, 1956.

LAGERKVIST, PÄR. *Barabbas*. New York: Random House, 1951.

LAGERLÖF, SELMA. *Memories of My Childhood: Further Years at Mårbacka*. New York: Doubleday, Doran, 1934.

———. *The Miracles of Antichrist*. Translated from the Swedish by Paulini Bancroft Flach. London: Gay & Bird, 1899.

LAKE, ALEXANDER. *The Past and the Future of the Croft Easter Lily*. Lompoc, California: Flower World Press, 1947.

LAMKIN, NINA B. *Easter and the Spring*. New York: Samuel French, 1935.

La Rousse Encyclopedia of Mythology. New York: Prometheus Press, 1959.

LAVERTY, MAURA. *Feasting Galore: Recipes and Food Lore from Ireland*. New York: Holt, Rinehart & Winston, 1961.

LEHNER, ERNST AND JOHANNA. *Folklore and Symbolism of Flowers, Plants and Trees*. New York: Tudor, 1960.

LIPKIND, WILLIAM. *Days to Remember: An Almanac*. New York: Obolensky, 1961.

MCKNIGHT, FELIX R. *The Easter Story*. New York: Holt, 1953.

MCSPADDEN, J. WALTER. *The Book of Holidays*. New York: Crowell, 1958.

MARIE, GRAND DUCHESS OF RUSSIA. *Education of a Princess: A Memoir*. New York: Viking, 1931.

MARSHALL, CATHERINE (ed.). Peter Marshall's "The First Easter." New York: McGraw-Hill, 1959.

MEYER, ROBERT, JR. *Festivals, U. S. A*. New York: Ives Washburn, 1950.

MILLER, MARY BRITTON. *A Handful of Flowers*. New York: Pantheon, 1959.

MILLER, SAMUEL H. *The Life of the Soul*. New York: Harper, 1951.

MINTER, JOHN EASTER. *The Chagres: River of Westward Passage*. New York: Rinehart, 1948.

MOLDENKE, HAROLD N. and ALMA L. *Plants of the Bible*. Waltham, Mass.: Chronica Botanica, 1952.

MONKS, JAMES L. *Great Catholic Festivals*. New York: Schuman, 1957.

MUNRO, DANA CARLETON, and SONTAG, RAYMOND JAMES. *The Middle Ages: 395–1500*. New York: Century, 1921.

NASH, ELIZABETH TODD. *One Hundred and One Legends of Flowers*. Boston: Christopher House, 1927.

NEWLAND, MARY REED. *The Year and Our Children*. New York: Kenedy, 1956.

NORTHALL, G. F. *English Folk-Rhymes.* London: Kegan Paul, 1892.

NUTT, ALFRED. *Studies of the Legend of the Holy Grail.* London: David Nutt, 1888.

O'CALLAGHAN, SEAN. *The Easter Lily.* New York: Roy, 1958.

OPIE, IONA and PETE. *The Lore and Language of School Children.* New York: Oxford, 1959.

PARMELEE, ALICE. *All the Birds of the Bible, Their Stories, Identification and Meaning.* New York: Harper, 1959.

PRESSE, G. W. STEPTIMUS. *The Art of Perfumery and the Methods of Obtaining the Odors of Plants.* Philadelphia: Lindsay and Blakiston, 1867.

PRATT, ANNE, and MILLER, THOMAS. *The Language of Flowers, the Association of Flowers, Popular Tales of Flowers.* London: Simpkin, Marshall, Hamilton, Kent, 1892.

QUINN, VERNON. *Stories and Legends of Garden Flowers.* New York: Stokes, 1939.

RADFORD, EDWIN. *Unusual Words and How They Came About.* New York: Philosophical Library, 1946.

———, and MONA A. *Encyclopaedia of Superstitions.* New York: Philosophical Library, 1949.

ROBB, DAVID M., and GARRISON, J. J. *Art in the Western World.* New York: Harper, 1953.

ROBINSON, HERBERT SPENCER, and WILSON, KNOX. *Myths and Legends of All Nations.* New York: Garden City Books, 1960.

SACKVILLE-WEST, V. *The Easter Party.* London: Michael Joseph, 1951.

SCHAUFFLER, ROBERT HAVEN (ed.). *Easter: Its History, Celebration, Spirit and Significance as Related in Prose.* Compiled by Susan Tracy Rice. New York: Moffat, Yard, 1916.

SCHERMAN, DAVID E., and WILCOX, RICHARD. *Literary England.* New York: Random House, 1944.

SELSAM, MILLICENT E. *Plants that Heal.* New York: Morrow, 1959.

SHACKLETON, ROBERT. *The Book of Washington.* Philadelphia: Penn. Pub. Co., 1922.

SHOEMAKER, ALFRED L. *Eastertide in Pennsylvania: A Folk Cultural Study.* Kutztown, Pennsylvania: Pennsylvania Folklife Society, 1960.

SKINNER, CHARLES M. *Myths and Legends Beyond Our Borders.* Philadelphia: Lippincott, 1899.

SMITH, H. A. *Lyric Religion, the Romance of Immortal Hymns.* New York: Revell, 1931.

SMITH, HERMAN. *Sting: The Story of a Cook.* New York: Barrows, 1946.

SPICER, DOROTHY GLADYS. *Feast-Day Cakes from Many Lands.* New York: Holt, Rinehart & Winston, 1960.

STERMAN, PHYLLIS. *Sweet Sixteen Cook Book.* New York: Sterling, 1952.

STOKER, FRED. *A Book of Lilies.* London: Penguin Books, 1943.

Sunset Books and *Sunset Magazine.* Menlo Park, California: Lane Pub. Co.

SWAYNE, AMELIA W. *The Observance of Easter.* Philadelphia: Religious Education Committee, Friends General Conference.

TAYLOR, GLADYS. *Saints and Their Flowers.* London: Mowbray, 1956.

TEALE, EDWIN WAY. *Green Treasury.* New York: Dodd, Mead, 1952.

———. *North with the Spring.* New York: Dodd, Mead, 1951.

THORNTON, FRANCIS BEAUCHESNE. *The Donkey Who Always Complained: A Parable for Moderns.* New York: Kenedy, 1956.

TOOR, FRANCES. *Festivals and Folkways of Italy.* New York: Crown, 1953.

———. *A Treasury of Mexican Folkways.* Mexico: Mexico Press, 1947.

A Treasure of Easter Religious Art. Milwaukee: Ideals Pub. Co., 1960.

TUBBY, RUTH P. *A Picture Dictionary of the Bible.* New York: Abingdon-Cokesbury, 1949.

URLIN, ETHEL L. *Festivals, Holy Days and Saints' Days.* London: Simpkin, Marshall, Hamilton, Kent, 1915.

VAN BUREN, MAUD, and BEMIS, KATHARINE ISABEL. *Easter in Modern Story.* New York: Century, 1929.
VAN LOON, HENDRIK. *The Story of Mankind.* New York: Garden City Pub., 1938.
VAN TREECK, CARL, and CROFT, ALOYSIUS. *Symbols in the Church.* Milwaukee: Bruce, 1960.
VANN, GERALD. *The Paradise Tree.* New York: Sheed & Ward, 1959.
WALKER, WINIFRED. *All the Plants of the Bible.* New York: Harper, 1957.
WALSH, WILLIAM S. *Curiosities of Popular Customs.* Phila.: Lippincott, 1897.
Washington, City and Capitol. Washington, D.C.: U.S. Gvt. Ptg. Off., 1937.
WATERMAN, PHILIP F. *The Story of Superstition.* New York: Grosset, 1929.
WEISER, FRANCIS X. *The Easter Book.* New York: Harcourt, Brace, 1954.
———. *Handbook of Christian Feasts and Customs.* New York: Harcourt, Brace, 1952.
———. *The Holy Day Book.* New York: Harcourt, Brace, 1956.
WELLS, H. G. *The Outline of History.* New York: Macmillan, 1921.
WEST, JESSAMYN. *The Friendly Persuasion.* New York: Harcourt, Brace, 1943.
WHITE, T. H. *The Bestiary, A Book of Beasts.* New York: Putnam, 1960.
WILSON, ADELAIDE. *Flower Arranging for Churches.* New York: Barrows, 1952.
WINKWORTH, CATHERINE. *Christian Singers of Germany.* New York: Macmillan.
WINZEN, DAMASUS. *Symbols of Christ.* New York: Kenedy, 1955.
World Almanac and Book of Facts, The. New York: N. Y. World-Telegram & The Sun, 1961.
WRIGHT, RICHARDSON. *A Book of Days for Christians.* Philadelphia: Lippincott, 1951.

Books for Children About Easter

ANON. *The Art of Beatrix Potter.* New York: Warne, 1955.
BELPRÉ, PURA. *The Tiger and the Rabbit.* Boston: Houghton Mifflin, 1946.
BROWN, MARGARET WISE. *The Golden Egg Book.* New York: Simon & Schuster, 1947.
BURGESS, THORNTON W. *Adventures of Peter Cottontail.* Boston: Little, Brown, 1912.
———. *Now I Remember.* Boston: Little, Brown, 1960.
COATSWORTH, ELIZABETH. *Twelve Months Make a Year.* New York: Macmillan, 1943.
CONOVER, CHARLOTTE. *A Holiday Story Sampler.* Chicago: Whitman, 1941.
HARPER, WILHELMINA (Ed.). *Easter Chimes: Stories for Easter and the Spring Season.* New York: Dutton, 1942.
HARRIS, JOEL CHANDLER. *Uncle Remus.* New York: Appleton-Century, 1892.
HAYES, WILMA P. *Easter Fires.* New York: Coward McCann, 1959.
HAZELTINE, ALICE ISABEL, and SMITH, ELVA SOPHRONIA (Eds.). *The Easter Book of Legends and Stories.* New York: Lothrop, Lee & Shepard, 1947.
HEYWARD, DUBOSE. *The Country Bunny and The Little Gold Shoes: As Told to Jenifer.* Boston: Houghton Mifflin, 1939.
JUNIOR PRESS (Eds.). *Happy Easter Stories: Story-Hour Tales from Junior Press Editions.* Chicago: Whitman, 1926.
LAGERLÖF, SELMA. *Christ Legends.* New York: Holt, 1908.
LAWSON, ROBERT. *Rabbit Hill.* New York: Viking, 1956.

LILLIE, AMY MORRIS. *The Book of Three Festivals: Stories for Christmas, Easter and Thanksgiving.* New York: Dutton, 1948.

LLOYD, MARY EDNA. *Glad Easter Day.* New York: Abingdon, 1961.

MEYER, EDITH P. *The Three Guardsmen.* New York: Abingdon, 1960.

MILHOUS, KATHERINE. *The Egg Tree.* New York: Scribners, 1950.

PAULI, HERTHA. *The First Easter Rabbit.* New York: Ives Washburn, 1961.

POLITI, LEO. *Song of the Swallows.* New York: Scribners, 1949.

POTTER, BEATRIX. *The Tale of Peter Rabbit.* New York: Warne, 1908.

RATHBUN, HELEN K. *Easter Surprise.* New York: Crowell, 1947.

SECHRIST, ELIZABETH HOUGH, and WOOLSEY, JANETTE. *It's Time for Easter.* Philadelphia: Macrae-Smith, 1961.

SEREDY, KATE. *The Good Master.* New York: Viking, 1935.

TOOR, FRANCES. *The Golden Carnation and Other Stories Told in Italy.* New York: Lothrop, Lee & Shepard,1960.

TUBBY, RUTH P. *A Picture Dictionary of the Bible.* New York: Abingdon-Cokesbury, 1949.

Index

Abbé d' Auteroche, 75
Abel, 94
Adam, 23, 24, 93, 94
Adventures of Peter Cottontail, 42
Aesculapius, 34
Africa, 13
Agnus Dei, 71
Agony in the Garden, 89
Ajax Mountain, 102
Alaska, 99
Ale, 65
Alexandria, 8, 41
All the Birds of the Bible, 29
Allah, 34
Allen, Edgar F., 97
Allen, Homer, 97
Alvarado Canyon, 104
America, 19, 20, 32, 42, 52, 72, 98, 105
America the Beautiful, 105
American Orchid Society Bulletin, 17
Anastasius, 35
Animals, cake, 72
Annunciation, the, 33
Antioch, 95
Aphrodite, 41
Apollo, 33
Apostles, 24, 25
Aquinas, Thomas, 68, 69
Arabia, 13, 36
Archaeologia, 35
Ark of the Covenant, 11
Armenia, 71
Armenians, 24
Artichokes, 57
Ash Wednesday, 46, 48, 81, 83, 84, 87

Aspen, Colorado, 102
Ass, 39
Austria, 48, 70, 87

Bacon, 45, 56
Bailey, Carolyn S., 109
Bailey, Temple, 118
Banana, 52
Bannock Tuesday, 46
Baptism, 90
Barabbas, 4
Barrel, 79
Basil of Antioch, 95
Basket, 78
Bates, Katharine Lee, 105
Bavaria, 90
Bede, 7
Bells, 75, 87, 105
Bennu bird, 67
Bermuda, 20, 21
Bethlehem, 39
Bethlehem, Pennsylvania, 56, 103
Bethune, Ade, 42
Bible, Vulgate, 31
de Bienville, Jean Baptiste, 81
Biloxi, Mississippi, 82
Binsa-graws, 73
Bird of Consolation, 32
Bird, Easter egg, 73
   Savior, 31
Blessed Sacrament, 88
Blossom Sunday, 85
Boats, sailing, 89
Bogg, 80
Bolton, Ivy, 110
Book of Common Prayer, 84
Book of Washington, 73
Busio, Jacomo, 14

Boston, 19
Brahma, 68
Branch Sunday, 85
Brandon, Oregon, 21
Brandt, John, 50
Brazil, 19, 75
Bread, 88
Bre'r Rabbit Tales, 42
British Museum, 71
Britons, 10
Brittany, 12
Bulgaria, 90
Bunny, 43
   toys, 42
Buns, hot cross, 89
Burgess, Thorton W., 42
Burying of the Sardine, 46, 8
Butter, 84
Butter Week, 80
Butterfly, 36, 73

Cadillac Mountain, 102
Caesar, 3, 94
Caiaphas, 29
Cake, 42, 75
   Easter, 78
Calico, 73
California, 21, 102
Calvary, 4, 10, 12, 15, 32, 10
Camelot, 95
Campo Santo, 12
Canada, 78
Candies, 42
Candle, Paschal, 80, 89, 90
Candles, 88, 90
Canejo, 41
Capistrano, California, 33
Carling Sunday, 52
Carlings, 52

135

Carnival, 80, 81
Carol singing, 86
Carolinas, the, 78
Carols, 90
Cathedral of the Pines, 104
Cathedral of Sofia, 90
Central Park, New York, 74
Ceremony of the Cart, 90
Ceres, 13
Chare Sunday, 85
Charlemagne, 10
Charoseth, 65
Cheese, 84, 87
Chesire, 15
Chesterton, G. K., 39
Chicago, 99
Chicken, 34, 72
Child Jesus, 24
Christ-Kindel, 78
Christianity, banner of, 26
Christmas, 8, 10, 11, 20, 25, 42, 43, 79, 80, 95
Christmas Eve, 78
Christos Voskresse, 64, 71, 76
Church, at St. Croce, 88
  Moravian, 56
  Russian Orthodox, 64
Civil War, 78
Clark, Margery, 49
Clement, Marguerite, 122
Clement, St., 35
Cleopas, 6
Cleveland Plain Dealer, 99
Cloister Collection, The, 95
Clothes, new, 90
Cock, 2, 33, 34
Cock-fighting, 34
Coffee, 73
Collins, Rev. R. C., 47
Collop Monday, 45
Comus, 81, 82
Constantine, 41
Contests, egg-rolling, 68
Cookies, 42, 71
Corcoran Art Gallery, 76
Corinthians, Epistle to the, 35
Corn, 54
Costain, Thomas B., 95
Council of Nicea, 8, 41
Creoles, 81
Crippled Child, The, 98
Croft, Sidney, 21
Crossbill, 29, 32
Crosses, 71
Crow, 90
Crown of Thorns, 9, 10, 11, 15, 24, 26, 30–32, 35, 39, 41, 70, 75, 94, 104
Crusades, 12, 53, 69, 74
Custard, baked, 65
Czechoslovakia, 27, 38, 53, 80

David, 24, 36
Day, of the Green Ones, 86–87
  of Judgment, 34
  of Whipping, 27
Death Valley, 102
Deer, 70
Demons, 79
Denmark, 27
Denver, 102
Devil, the, 33, 37, 40
Dice-throwing, 89
Distel-finks, 73
District of Columbia, 99
Donahey, J. H., 99
Donkey, 37, 38
Donkey Who Always Complained, The, 39
Donkey's Glory, 39
Doves, 33, 35, 90, 94, 95
Druids, 25
Duomo, the, 90

Eagle, 33, 35, 36
Easter, Its Story and Meaning, 68
Easter Book, The, 42, 69, 83, 85
Easter bread, 75
Easter bunnies, 41, 42, 97
Easter cake, 34
Easter dates, 7
Easter Day, 75, 89, 101
Easter egg-rolling contest, 74
Easter eggs, 34, 41, 76
  candy, 34
Easter Eve, 56, 64, 78, 89, 90, 103
  vigil of, 90
Easter Fire, 41, 75
Easter goddess, 41
Easter greetings, 90
Easter hens, 72
Easter Island, 102
Easter lambs, 38
Easter letter, 90
Easter Man, burning of the, 90
Easter, meaning of, 7
Easter Monday, 27, 73, 90
Easter morning, 75, 102
Easter parade, 74
Easter rabbit, 78
Easter Saturday, 38, 80, 87, 89
Easter Seal Research Foundation, 99
Easter Seal Societies, 99
Easter Sunday, 47, 73, 77, 102
  sunrise service, 102, 104
Easter-tree, 72
Easter Week, 69, 85, 102
Eastertide, 65
  in Pennsylvania, 48, 78
Ecclesiastes, 11
Edward I, 71

Egg Saturday, 45
Egg Tree, The, 72
Egg(s), 34, 43, 77, 78, 84
  candy, 68, 71
  colored, 70, 75, 78, 91
  decoration of, 73
  designed, 70
  duck, 75
  Easter, 41, 42, 64, 67, 90
  golden, 67
  goose, 75
  hard-boiled, 75
  Mundane, 67
  pace, 70
  painted, 77
  pickled, 70
  roasted, 65
  strained, 70
  Vienna Easter, 71
  Wooden, 74
Eggshells, 72, 77
  boats of, 77
Egypt, 7, 11, 24, 25, 35, 36, 39, 41, 67, 68
Elba, Island of, 19
Elephants, 73
Elijah cup, 66
Elizabeth, Queen, 86
Elyria, Ohio, 97, 98
Emmaus, 5
England, 10, 14, 19, 20, 35, 38, 88, 89
Eostre, 7, 41
Equinox, Spring, 8
Eucharist, 15
Eve, 23, 93, 94

Fabergé, Carl, 76, 77
Fastnachts, 45
Fat Days, 80
Fat Tuesday, 80
Father's Kingdom, 1
Feast of Feasts, The, 7, 8, 45
Feast of Meat, The, 7
Feast, movable, 8
  Paschal, 57
  of the Torches, 79–80
  of the Transfiguration, 24
Federal Vocational Rehabilitation Act, 98
Ferguson, George, 31
Fig Sunday, 52, 85
Figs, 52, 87
Finland, 38, 77
Fire(s), 77, 79, 80, 90
  Sunday, 79
  Easter, 75
Firecracker, 90
First Sunday of Lent, 80
First World War, 77
Fish, 71
Florence, Italy, 88, 90

[30

Florida, 26, 27, 54, 102
Flowering Sunday, 52, 85
Flowers (*See* Plants and Flowers)
Fowls of God, 10
France, 10, 19, 74, 75, 79, 88, 94, 101
Franklin, Ben, 65
Fredericksburg, Texas, 75
French Guiana, 15
Friar, 42
Friday of Mourning, 88

Galilee, 2, 3, 5
Gammon, 56
Gander, 68, 69
Garden of Eden, 23, 24, 26, 35, 93
Garden of the Gods at Colorado Springs, 104
Garments, white, 90
Geb, 67, 68
Geese, 72
Geikié, Cunningham, 29
General's Easter Box, The, 118
Genesis, 23
George, St., 80
George V, 86
George Washington University, 102
Germany, 10, 25, 42, 48, 70–73, 77, 79, 87
Gethsemane, 2, 13, 15, 19, 25, 29, 30
Giorgione, 19
Glastonbury, England, 10, 95
Gloves, 90
God's Friday, 88
Golden Egg, The, 110
Goldfinch, 29, 31 [94
Good Friday, 54, 55, 77, 87–89,
Goodhall, Nan, 39
Goodies Day, 46
Golgotha, 27, 29, 30
Grand Canyon, 102
Grand Canyon National Park, 104
Grape juice, 87
Grapes, 87
Grapevine, 95
Great Britain, 10
Great Cackler, The, 68
Great Day, 7
Great Friday, 88
Great Night, 7
Greece, 25, 36, 41, 75, 85
Greeks, 24
Green Thursday, 52, 53, 86
Greens, dandelion, 45
Gregory the Great, 86
Guarore, 81
Gypsy, 89

Haggadah, 65
Half Moon Dome, 104
Hallel, 87
Halloween, 80
Hallowing of rings, 88
Ham, 45, 56
Hams and Eggs Show, 58
Hamsa, 68
Handbook of Christian Feasts and Customs, The, 83
Handful of Clay, A, 116
Hare, 41, 42
Hark, J. Max, 103
Harris, Joel Chandler, 42
Harris, Paul P., 98
Harris, William K., 20
Hasting's Dictionary of Christ and the Gospels, 65
Hawaii, 68, 99
Hebrews, 26
Hen, 34, 68, 72, 77
Henry VII, 50
Herbs, 52, 57, 65
Herculaneum, 55
Herod, 3, 25, 39
Herodias, 28
Herodotus, 36
Herring, 56
Hiring fairs, 50
History of Northumberland, 68
Hoatson, Florence, 34
Hodgenville, Kentucky, 104
Holboll, Eimer, 97
Hole, Christina, 34
Holkam Bible Picture Book, 31
Hollywood Bowl, 102, 104
Holy City, 29, 103
Holy Family, 9, 10, 12, 24, 25
Holy Friday, 88
Holy Ghost Shell, 40
Holy Grail, 74, 93, 94, 95
Holy Land, 9, 10, 12–14, 24, 25, 30, 37, 87
Holy Saturday, 56, 88, 90
Holy Sepulcher, 88
Holy Spirit, 33
Holy Thursday, 65, 84, 86
Holy Week, 17, 26, 55, 75
Honey, 33
Honolulu, 105
Hoop, 79
Hosanna Sunday, 85
Hot Cross buns, 89
Housman, A. E., 14
Hungary, 7
Hunting for eggs, 75

Idylls of the King, 95
IHS, 51
Illinois, 98
India, 35, 67, 68
Indians, Aztec, 104

International Society for Crippled Children, 99
Isabel Stewart Gardner Museum, 19
Israelites, 7, 11, 24
Israfil, 93, 94
Italy, 10, 34, 38

Jaazaniah, 34
Japan, 20
Jericho, 12
Jerome, St., 31
Jerusalem, 5, 6, 26, 29, 33, 39, 104
Jesus Hominum Salvator, 51
Joanna, 5
Job, 33, 36
John, St., 7, 8, 13, 33, 38, 89
John the Baptist, St., 28, 38, 40
Joseph, St., 24, 33, 39, 84
Joseph of Arimathea, 10, 94, 95
Josephine, Empress, 19
Journey to Siberia, 75
Judas, 1, 2, 15, 24, 27, 28, 53, 88, 89
Judases farina, 53
Judgment Hall, The, 104

Kaf Marjam, 12
Kalevala, 68
Kane, Hartnett, 82
Kentucky, 98
Key West, Florida, 102
King of Butchers, 81
King Momo, 81
King Solomon, 24
King, Paul H., 99
Kiss of Judas, 89
Kiss Thursday, 87
Kohl, 76
Koran, 34
Kundry, 28
Kutztown, Pennsylvania, 78

Laban, 39
Lagerlöf, Selma, 12, 30, 39
Lamb, 7, 33, 37, 52, 53, 72, 87
  of God, 7, 38, 71, 101
Lamps, 90
Lancashire, England, 65
Lancaster *Intelligencer*, 103
Last Supper, The, 1, 86, 87, 89, 93
Lawson, Robert, 42
Lawton, Oklahoma, 102
Legend of the Crossbill, The, 32
Lent, 45, 69
Lenten fast, 69, 80
Lenten season, 85
Leopard, 40
Lerner, Allan J., 95
Liberal, Kansas, 46

Life and Words of Christ, The,
    29
Lily, Easter, 19
Lion, 40
Loewe, Frederick, 95
Lohengrin, 95
Long Friday, 88
Longfellow, Henry Wadsworth,
    32
Lönnrot, Elias, 68
Lord's Day of Joy, 89
Lord's Supper, 104
Lothrop's Annual, 72
Love feast, 56
Lowery, Woodbury, 115
Lucifer, 93, 94
Luke, St., 3, 5, 31, 33, 34

Madagascar, 11, 14
Madison, James, 73
Magdalene, Mary, 5
Magpies, 10
Maine, 104
Major, Johannes, 32
Marbles, playing, 89
Mardi Gras, 46, 80, 81
Mark, St., 33, 40
Marseilles, France, 94
Mary, Virgin, 5, 24, 25, 39, 71
Matthew, St., 1, 33
Matzoths, 87
Maundy money, 86
Maundy Thursday, 42, 70, 86
Meal in the Upper Room, 87
Meat, 80
Mercury, 34
Messiah, 39, 85
Metropolitan Museum of Art,
    95
Mexico, 34, 86
Mi Negro, 81
Michael, 93
Mid-Lent, 50
Mid-Lent Sunday, 49
Middle Ages, 25, 36, 79, 95, 105
Midsummer, 80
Milhous, Katherine, 72
Milk, 84
Mirror Lake, 104
Mississippi, 82
Mistick Krewe, 82
Mizpah, 34
Mobile, Alabama, 82
Mohammedans, 24
Moldenke, Dr. Harold N., 14
Montuno, 81
Moravians, 102
Mormons, 24
Moror, 65
Mosen, Julius, 32
Moses, 6, 7, 94
Mothering Sunday, 49, 51

Mother's Day, 50
Mount Desert Island, Maine,
    102
Mount of Olives, 2, 25
Mount Roraima, 15
Mountain of Lebanon, 24
*Myths and Legends Beyond Our
    Borders,* 15

Napoleon, 19
National Brotherhood Sunday,
    28
National Cathedral, 10
National Gallery, 32
National Society for Crippled
    Children and Adults, 97, 98
Nazareth, 39
Nebuchadnezzar, 34
New Hampshire, 104
New Orleans, 81, 82
New York, 27, 78
Nicholas, St., 42
Nicodemus, 13
Noah, 33
Nut, 67

Oklahoma Oberammergau, 103
Old wife, 80
Old woman winter, 80
Olives, 87
Olney, England, 46
Once and Future King, The, 95
Onion Skins, 73
Ontario, 27
Oschter Haws, 78
Osiris, 67
Oster Eier, 72
Oster Hase, 72
Owl, 31

Pace-egging, 70
Painted rabbit, 41
Palestine, 10, 11, 13, 18, 27, 29,
    31, 33, 36, 37
Palm Sunday, 26, 27, 39, 52, 75,
    83, 85, 86, 102
Panama, 41, 81
Pancake, 46, 47
Pancake Bell, 46
Pancake Day, 46
Pancake Greeze, 46
Pancake racing, 46
Pancake Tuesday, 45
Paris, France, 81
Park of the Red Rocks, 102
Parmelee, Alice, 29
Parsifal, 28, 95
Party, Easter, 72
Pasch, 7
Paschal egg, 70
Paschal lamb, 38
Paschal season, 42

Pasche, 71
Pasqua Florida, 102
Passion, 88
Passion play, 89
Passover, 1, 7, 8, 26, 38, 65, 68,
    87, 94
Passover Thanksgiving Prayer,
    87
Passover Week, 85
Paste eggs, 71
Peacock, 35, 67
Pelican, 31, 69
Pennsylvania, 78, 98
Pennsylvania Dutch, 52, 72, 73,
    77, 78
Pennsylvania Folklife Society,
    78
Penny, Prudence, 65
Persia, 13
Peter, 2, 5, 15, 33
Phoenix, 35, 36, 67, 69
Picking eggs, 73
Pig, 40
Pigeon, 90
Piggy banks, 40
Pike, 40
Pike's Peak, Colorado, 105
Pilate, 3, 4, 29, 89, 104
Pisa, 12
Plants and Flowers:
    Acacia, 11
    Aloe, 13
    Anacardium occidentale, 11
    Anastatica hierochuntica, 12
    Anemone coronaria, 11, 18
    Barberry, 10
    Berberis vulgaris, 10
    Blue Vervain, American, 12
    Box thorn, 10
    Bramble, 10
    Brier, 9
    Broom, Butcher's, 11
    Burnet, spiny, 11
    Cactus, Easter-lily, 19
    Capavris spinosa, 10
    Cashew, 11
    Cayenne, 15
    Century plant, 13
    Christ Thorn, The, 11
    Crataegus oxycathana, 10
    Crocus, 10
    Crown of Thorns, 9, 11, 15
    Crown imperial, 12
    Cyclamen, 13
    Daffy-down-dilly, 13
    Dove orchid, n 16
    Easter lily, 13, 20
    Easter orchid, 15
    Easter rose, 13
    El Espirito Santo, 16
    English holly, 9
    Epidendrum atropurpureum, 18

Plants and Flowers—(continued)
  Euphorbia splendens, 11
  Flower of the Holy Spirit, 16
  Flower of the Martyrs, 10
  Fritillary, 12
  Geranium, Martha Washington, 19
  Glastonbury thorn, 10
  Golden trumpets, 14
  Hawthorn, 10, 11
  Herb of the Cross, 12
  Herbs, 86, 87
  Hibiscus syriacus, 10
  Holy Ghost plant, 16, 17
  Holy thorn, 10
  Hyacinth, 18, 43
  Ilex aquifolium, 9
  Ivy, 11
  Larkspur, 13
  Lilium Harrisi, 20
  Lily, 19, 20
    Calla, 104
    Croft, 21
    Easter, 41, 97, 99
    Lent, 13, 14
    madonna, 20
    of the field, 11, 14
    of-the-valley, 12
    red, 20
  Lycium europaeum, 10
  Madder, root, 73
  Mary's hand, 12
  Myrrh, 13, 36
  Narcissus, 10, 14, 18
  Oleander, 10
  Orchid, 18
  Orchis maculata, 15
  Palestine tumbleweed, 12
  Paliurus spina-christi, 11
  Passiflora, 14
  Passion flower, 14
  Poinsettia, 20, 41
  Pomegranate, 13
  Prickly-rush, 11
  Resurrection flower, 12
  Ressurrection plant, 12
  Rosa-Mariae, 12
  Rose, 9, 10, 30
    of Jericho, 12
    of Sharon, 10
    of the Virgin, 12
  Rubus coronaricus, 9
  Rubus fruticosus, 10
  Ruscus, 11
  Ruscus aculeatus, 11
  Semana Santá, 17, 18
  Shittah-tree, 11
  Tansy, 58
  Tears of Mary, 12
  Tulip, 10, 18, 19, 73
  Verbena, 12
  Verbena hastata, 12

Plants and Flowers—(continued)
  Veronica, 12
  Violets, 50
  Wild daffodil, 13, 14
  Wild hyssop, 10
  Wild orchid, 15
  Willow, 11
  Wind flower, 11, 12
Plants of the Bible, 14
Pliny, 35
Pluto, 13
Poland, 48, 75
Polish tradition, 25
Polito, Leo, 33
Pollero, 81
Pomeranian tradition, 25
Pomläzka, 27
Ponce de Leon Finds the Land of Flowers, 115
Portugal, 34
Potter, Beatrix, 42
Pottery, 89
Prajapati, 67
Preston, Margaret Thornington, 16
Pretzels, 45, 48
Proserpine, 13
Provence, 75
Psalm 83:13, 12
Psalm 102:6, 31
Ptah, 67
Pudding, fig, 85
  gooseberry, 67
Puerto Rico, 99
Punchbowl National Memorial Cemetery, 105
Purdan, M. A., 17
Purification rite, 27
Puritans, 10
Pysanki, 70

Quaker, 78
Queen New Orleans, City by the River, 82
Quinquagesima Sunday, 45

Rabbit, 13, 37, 41, 43, 72
Rabbit Hill, 42
Rapallo, Italy, 86
Recipes:
  Avgolemono, 60
  Bábovka, 59
  Beránek, 53
  Biscuit, Naples, 57
  Blanc Mange, Easter, 62
  Bread, coffee, 59
    Czechoslovakian yeast, 56
    Easter, 55
    Grecian Feast, 60
    Orange, 49
  Buns, hot cross, 5

Recipes—(continued)
  Cake, car, 47
    cheese, 59
    coffee, 55
    Daffodil, 63
    Easter, 57
    Easter Lamb, 53, 54
    Irish Lenten, 49
    Lamb variation, 53
    mothering, 50
    plum, 65
    Russian Easter, 64
    Simnel, 45, 50, 51
  Car-cake, 47
  Cinnamon rabbits, 63
  Coffee-cake, 59
  Collop, 45
  Easter bunnies, 63
  Easter chick, 63
  Egg collops, 46
  Eggs, Gefillte, 66
  Fastnacht, 47
  Fastnacht Kuche, 48
  Frosting, Glacé, for simnel cake, 51
    seven-minute, 54
  Furmety, 45, 51
  Ham, baked, 61
    Easter, 57
  Ice cream Easter bunnies, 64
  Icing, boiled, 57
  Karpas, 66
  Kulich, 45, 64
  Kulichi, 64
  Lamb, crown roast of, 58
    roast, 59
  Lenten soup, 48
  Marzipan, 51
  Matzoth, 65
  Mäyiritsä, 60
  Mayvutsa, 45
  Mazanec, 56, 59
  Muffins, poppy seed, 49
  Pasha, 64
  Pasta Frolla, 59, 60
  Paste, Almond, 51
  Pie, Easter eggnog, 62
    Italian Easter, 59, 60
  Posna zupa, 45
  Postna zupa, 48
  Pudding, fig, 45, 52
    Tansy, 57, 58
  Rolls, Passover, 66
  Sauce, cider, 62
    cranberry-raisin, for ham, 61
    mustard, 61
    orange, 62
  Shrovetide pancakes, 47
  Soup, Good Friday, 56
  Toddy, egg, 56
  Wafers, mid-Lent, 51
Renaissance, 36

Resurrection, The, 5, 7, 8, 12, 13, 24, 25, 32, 35, 41, 43, 67, 69, 71, 76, 101, 105
Rice, 87
Richard Symond's Diary, 50
Richmond, Maine, 64
Robin, 10, 29–31
Roggeveen, 102
Rolling eggs, 73
Romans, 26
Rome, 36, 75, 85
Rooster, 34, 70
Rope, skipping, 89
Rotary International, 98
Round Table, 94
Russia, 75–77

St. Peter's, 85, 86
St. Petersburg, 76
St. Veronica's Handkerchief, 12
Sainte Chapelle, Paris, 11
Salt Lake City, Utah, 104
San Diego, 104
Sand dollar, 40
San Juan Mission, 33
Sangraal, 94
Sanskrit, 41
Sargent, Mrs. Thomas P., 20
Satan, 31
Schwenckfeld, 32
Scotland, 75
Scratch-carving, 73
Sea of Galilee, 31
Seal, Easter, 97, 99
Seder, The, 66
Seminole Indian Reservation, 27
Seth, 24
Setting for Passover, 65
Seven Last Words, 88
Shackleton, Robert, 73
Shakespeare, 27
Sheba, Queen of, 24
Shellfish, catching, 89
Shepherd, 37
Shepherds of Norfolk, The, 61
Shere Sunday, 85
Shier or Sher Thursday, 87
Shoemaker, Alfred L., 48, 78
Shrove Tuesday, 45–48, 79, 81
Shrovetide, 34, 45
Siberia, 77
Sicily, 85
Siege Perilous, 94
Signs and Symbols of Christian Art, 31
Silkworm, 86
Silver Chalice, The, 95
Simnel, 50, 51
Simnel, Lambert, 50
Simon, 4
Siroo, Joseph R., 102
Skinner, Charles M., 15, 28

Snowman, A. Kenneth, 76
Social Security Act, 99
Society for Prevention of Cruelty to Animals, The, 42
Solemnity of Solemnities, 7
Somerset County, Maryland, 58
Song of the Swallows, 33
South America, 15
South Carolina, 26
Spain, 27, 84, 89
Spanish Sunday, 85
Sparrow, 29
Spinach, 87
Spring, 80
Spring equinox, 70
Spun sugar, 38
Squirrels, 88
Stag, 70
Star of Bethlehem, 41
Stephens, George, 35
Straw man, 80
Sugar Egg, The, 109
Sun, rising of the, 105
Sun dance, 101
Sunday of the Palm Carrying, 85
Sunrise service, 97, 105
Swallows, 10, 29, 32, 33
Sweden, 56, 77, 90
Swifts, 29
Switzerland, 73
Syria, 12

Tactitus, 35
Tale of Peter Rabbit, 42
Tamborito, 81
Tampa, Florida, 104
Tart, cheese, 65
Temple of the Sun, 36
Tennessee, 78, 98
Tennyson, Alfred, Lord, 95
Texas, 27, 75
Theriotropheum Silesiae, 32
Thornton, Francis Beauchesne, 39
Three Hours, 88
Tiepolo's *Madonna of the Goldfinch*, 32
Tinsel, 72
Toldos, 81
Topcake, 65
Torches, 90
Toys, 75
Tree, Christmas, 72, 78
  Easter egg, 72
  of Knowledge, 23
  of Life, 23, 24, 26
Tree-frolic, 72
Trees:
  Alder, 25
  Alder catkins, 73
  Apple, 23

Trees—(*continued*)
  Apricot, 23
  Aspen, 24, 25
  Banana, 23
  Beech, 80
  Birch, 27
  Boxwood, 85
  Cabbage palmetto, 26
  Carob tree, 27
  Cedar, 24, 26
    of Lebanon, 24, 30
    red, 24
  Citron, 23
  Clematis, 25
  Cypress, 24, 26
  Date palm, 23, 26
  Dogwood, 26
  Elder, 24, 25
    black, 27
  Fig, 23, 25, 27
  Fir, 80, 86
  Glastonbury thorn, 95
  Hawthorn, 30
  Hickory bark, 73
  Judas berries, 27
  Judas tree, 27
  Juniper, 24, 25
  Juniperus communis, 24
  Mistletoe, 25
  Mountain ash, 23
  Oak, 24, 26
    holm, 25
  Olive, 24–26, 85, 86
  Palm, 23, 24, 26, 27, 88
    dates, 85
  Pear, 24, 25
  Pine, 24, 25
  Pomegranate, 23
  Poplar, 25, 27
  Populus tremula, 25
  Quercus ilex, 25
  Red-bud, 27
  Rose, brier, 27
  Sambucus nigra, 25
  Saw Palmetto, 26
  Serenoa repens, 26
  Tamarisk, 27
  Terebinth, 27
  Walnut, shells, 73
  Willow, 27, 28, 85, 86, 88
    Pussy, 28, 86
    sallow, 27
    Weeping, 27
  Yew, 85
Trees, egg, 68
Trottemeno, 39
Tuileries, the, Paris, 19
Turkey, 72
Twelfth Night, 79, 81

Ukko, 68
Ukraine, 75

Umberto, Bishop of Pisa, 12
United States, 11, 21, 26–28, 38, 42
Upper Marlboro, 58
Upper Room, The, 104
Urlin, Ethel L., 89
Usra, 41

Van Dyke, Henry, 116
Vatican, 15
Veal, roast, 65
Venice, 40
de Vert, Pierre, 15
Vespasian, 94
Victoria, Queen, 86
de Villegas, Emanuel, 14
Violet, 19
Virgin Islands, 72
Virginia, 78

Wales, 52
Walnuts, 87
Wandering Jew, legend of, 28
Washing of the feet, 86
Washington, D. C., 10, 73, 76
Water-Mother, 68
Watts, Alan W., 68
Wearyall Hill, 10
Weiser, Francis X., 42, 69, 83, 85
West Indies, 11
West Virginia, 98
Westminster Abbey, 86
Whale, 40
Wheel, 79
White, T. B., 95
Whitehouse, 73, 74
Whitsuns, 65
Why Robin Redbreast Sings at Easter Time, 30
Wichita Mountains, 103

William, the Conqueror, 37, 56
Willow-twig Sunday, 85
Winchester Museum, 51
Winston-Salem, North Carolina, 56, 102
Winter, 79, 80
Wise Men, The, 15
Witch, 77, 80, 90
Wooden clappers, 87
World-egg, 67, 68

X, B, 64
X, V, 71

Yellow, 34
Yosemite National Park, 104
Ys and Her Bells, 122

Zebedee, 2
Zedekiah, 34

Priscilla Sawyer Lord

an enthusiastic collector of Easter lore since her student days at Boston University, has pursued her hobby while traveling extensively on this continent and in Europe. She often uses her collection of Easter decorations to illustrate lectures. An accomplished book reviewer and narrator, she has made frequent contributions to newspapers and magazines and has participated in many radio programs. Mrs. Lord resides at Marblehead Neck, Massachusetts, with her husband and two daughters.

Daniel J. Foley

writer, lecturer and horticulturist, is the author of nine books, including *Christmas in the Good Old Days, Ground Covers for Easier Gardening, The Christmas Tree,* and *Little Saints of Christmas,* all of which have received wide acclaim in the press and on radio and television. From 1951–1957, Mr. Foley served as Editor of *Horticulture,* America's oldest garden magazine. A frequent contributor to newspapers and periodicals, a participant in radio and television programs, he lectures extensively on a variety of subjects. His interest in Easter customs and traditions is an outgrowth of his enthusiasm for holiday symbolism.